WHAT IF?

REGINA HOLLINGSWORTH

TABLE OF CONTENTS

INTRODUCTION

"What if" is a normal phrase spoken or thought after events have already finished. In this space, it generally means if only things had started and headed in another direction. At that moment, it is a statement of regret. In the case of preplanning, saying "What if" is great. Only then do you realize that you have options from which to choose from. But, after things are over these two words stand in the mind of the receiver's devastation because no other opportunities were presented. The decision was made and those involved seem like victims of circumstance. It just does not seem fair. This is the platform from where this writing will stand. You have come out, the circumstances could not be changed and you are left with the next best thought, "Where do I go from here?"

Before you can decide your next plan of action, it is normal to go through a myriad of unfruitful mindsets. "Why did these things happen to me? Whoever made the choices could not have understood how the circumstances would affect my life." These are not strange words. But, you have to learn how to maneuver with the circumstances just the way they are. There is a way to win no matter where you find yourself in life. The lifestyle of your parents will affect you. When you came to the age of knowing yourself, here you are. Your family's financial status, the neighborhood where you live, religious practices taught or modeled before you, as well as the make-up of your family are all bricks laid without your consent. Contemplating how each part will fit into your life will all be discussed in this book. Nothing happened to you; things happened around you and the negative can be overcome. Let all the thoughts, negative and otherwise, play out till they lead to peace.

Unless you live alone on a deserted island, throughout life you will come up against decisions made by participants in your various relationships that await your response. You can decide to react or respond, and yes there is a difference. Your spouse accepts a job in another state, makes a large item purchase without consulting you or you come home from work to face unexpected dinner guests. The deserted island looks promising right about now.

Life's plot thickens at every turn. You give your friend a ride to the convenience store and unbeknownst to you, it gets robbed. The judge does not buy your story and you get time for being an accomplice. You just bought your house and your employer says that your position is being transferred to a state one thousand miles away. Oh, life contains many twists and turns and you are right in the middle to answer to the aftereffects.

You did not choose your race, your parents, siblings, extended family, neighborhood, or economic status in which you were born. These are givens. But even with the worst situations, you have personal choices. No matter where you find yourself you have the opportunity to foster a different life if you do not like your present condition. You do not control the details of the pre-painted picture, but you do have authority over how you use the details to benefit your life and ultimately the destiny designed for you.

Now that you understand the whys of this writing, get a pen and paper to take notes. Open your heart and mind and prepare for the great things that must happen because you are receiving the tools for the better. You were built for what you are facing, what you have already encountered and will encounter in your future. Knowing that it is all part of what is called living, gives you a greater sense of, "I can do this!" This is the identical happenstance that everyone walks into as a result of being born. Use this book as one of the tools along with the success you see all around you. Everybody faces obstacles whether they are rich, poor, incapacitated to a degree, or simply have taken on too much for one person to handle. The day you come to yourself and are keenly aware of your course, it is time to say, "What if" and add the words, "I do this!" Your words and actions can turn the whys of your life into positive affirmations for your future decisions.

Where do you go from here? Up is your direction if you plan your life with the "givens" as your beginnings that have little influence on how you spend your future. Choose some "What ifs" until one works. *Here* is part of your journey, keeping going.

DEDICATION

This Book is dedicated to my two lovely daughters, Chanel and Chantel! I am proud and honored to be their mother! I cannot imagine life without you two in it! I love you MORE! This book is also dedicated to three "Sheroes" who have transitioned from this earthly life and now are awaiting their eternal reward, Michele Hollingsworth, Delores Rickenbacker, and Lucille Romona Phillips. These three women were sent by God to change my life forever at pivotal moments that you will read about later on in this book.

WHAT IF

What if I turn right not left

What if I said yes and not no

What if I decided to have Faith and Not Fear?

What If I lived my Dreams?

What If I asked Again?

What if I looked again?

What If I knocked Again?

What if I tried Again?

What if I

What if I

What if I

It haunts me

I will never know now

I can't let it go

I caused the pain

I lost everything

Am at a crossroad

Can I turn around?

Can I try again?

Do I get a Makeover?

Do I get another chance?

Is it too late?

Where do I go from here?

Let me let go

Can I let go

Want to let go

I want to be free of all the What Ifs

What if I had more time?

What if I could start over again?

What if I kept silent?

What if I spoke up?

What If

What If

What If

What If I made a different decision

What if I took that risk

What if I gave love a chance

What if I won the lottery

What if I forgave

What If

What If

What If

I may never know

What If

Chapter One

GOD IS IN CONTROL

I have found a place that answers all my questions of what if things had been different. Since I began to walk with God, peace has always come from the words that come alive from the Bible. These comforting words let me know, beyond any doubt, that God is in control. I want to share with you the mystery of my peace because it has proven to work for me time after time. I would be remiss if I do not share these keys with you.

Here are a few scriptures that are guaranteed to bring peace in the midst of any disruptions to your life. They are definite answers to your "What ifs?" They only can work if you affirmatively answer these questions. Do you believe the Bible? Is the Bible mere words to you, or just a book of stories? Let us face the truth, there are 66 Books in the Bible from Genesis to Revelation; the scriptures that you believe are the ones that will bring you an expected end. If you do not believe that God is the Great Physician, or that by His stripes you are healed; and God wants you in good health and all the other healing health scriptures in the Good Book then you will not ask Him to heal you. You will accept sickness, pain, and diseases as "givens" and they will become your own. If you do not believe in

Philippians 4:19 (NLT) that reads, "And the same God who takes care of "me" will supply all "my" needs from His glorious riches, which have been given to us in Christ Jesus", you will worry if your bills will get paid, if you will have food, clothing, and housing. God already told you in His word that if He provides food for the birds, how much more about you, are you not more valuable than birds? He will take care of you. All the words of God will manifest in your life, but you must mix them with your Faith that they will.

Now take a look at Romans 8:28 (AMP), "And we know [with great confidence] that God [who is deeply concerned about us] causes ALL things to work together [as a plan] for good for those who love God, to those who are called according to His plan and purpose." As a true Believer in Christ, not in man or woman or your Pastor or spouse or best friend, but as a Christ-like being, you must first know that whatever you are going through, is working for your good. The situation may not seem like it is working for your good. The odds may be against you but know that if you love God and are called according to His purpose and glory, He is working out the situation for your good. God will take what is meant to destroy you and give you a favorable outcome for His glory. He will take your tests and trials and turn them into a testimony if you truly love Him. God causes ALL things, not some things, not most things, but all circumstances to work together for your good if you love Him and are called according to His purpose and plan. You must ask yourself, "Do I love God," and, "Am I called according to His plan and purpose?"

"What if" the answers are yes to both questions? Then there is nothing in your life, good or bad that has happened to you or will happen to you that are not a part of God's plan "for" you. After accepting this truth, you will realize that what happened in your life or what is taking place in your present situation is working "for" you and not "to" you according to God's plans. He said, "For I know the plans I have "for" you declares the Lord, plans to prosper you and not "to" harm you, plans to give you hope and a future," (Jeremiah 29:11 NIV). God desires to give you hope and a future!

"What If" you began to realize that God is in control of your life? While you are sleep, God is not only working things out for you but He is also perfecting that which concerns you. God does not allow anything to happen to you that was not already predestinated, a part of His plans. Romans 8:30-31 goes on to say, "Moreover whom He did predestinate, them He also called: and who he called, them He also justified and whom He justified, them He also glorified. What shall we then say to these things? If God be for us, who can be against us?"

God wants to be in control of every aspect of your life! "What If" you made up in your mind today to let God be in control of your life and every situation. He wants to work all things out for your good because you do love Him and realize that you are called for His purpose and plan.

Then you have to come face to face with the next necessary question. How do you let God be in control of your life?

Proverbs 3:5-6 says (KJV), "Trust in the Lord with all your heart, lean not to your own understanding; in all your ways acknowledge Him and He shall direct your path."

Have faith that God knows what He is doing. His ways and thoughts are so much higher than ours. Isaiah 55: 8- 9 (NIV) reads like this, "For my thoughts are not your thoughts, neither are your ways my ways, declares the Lord. As the heavens are higher than the earth, so are my ways higher than your ways and my thoughts than your thoughts." This scripture assures us that God knows what He is doing. His thinking is better than ours when it comes to what is best for us and His ways and everything He allows is higher and better.

Deuteronomy 31:8 (NIV), "The Lord himself goes before you and will be with you; He will never leave you nor forsake you. Do not be afraid; do not be discouraged". Moses spoke these words to Joshua as he told Joshua not to be afraid to go into the Promised Land flowing with milk and honey that God was giving to the Israelites. Moses wanted Joshua to know that God was with him. God has not changed. God will never leave you or forsake you. God is well aware of all that has happened to you, and all that will happen to you according to His plan. You do not need to fear when you have God going ahead of your tomorrow.

Chapter Two

YOUR DECISIONS, YOUR CHOICES; YOU OWN IT

Did you ever wonder, "What If" Adam and Eve did not eat from the forbidden tree in the Garden of Eden (Genesis 3:6)? If they did not eat the fruit, would they still be alive and how would the world look like today? Now, that is some imagining. I guarantee the world could not look anything like it does today. It could not because it was these two that introduced sin into the world.

"What If" Cain never killed Abel (Genesis 4:8)? Some of the sermons that you have heard regarding this topic would never have been preached. Nobody could ever use any implication about giving from this story. The story would not have existed. Cain would most likely still have felt dejected that God did not receive his offering, but it was the murder of his brother that made all the difference.

"What if" Noah never built the Ark (Genesis 6:8-22)? This is a big one! If Noah never built the ark, he would probably have been mentioned in the Bible one time and not the 52 times that you can find his name. God used him and his family to represent the only ones who were an example of the kind of people He wanted the rest of His creation to be. But, God destroyed the rest of the world to show His anger with it. The majority of the mentions of Noah's name are to remind everyone else of the sovereignty of God. Noah building an ark in Genesis in the Old Testament is tied way into the New Testament describing the faith of one righteous man. The whole Bible would read a lot differently without Noah building the ark.

"What if" the people never attempted to build the tower of Babel (Genesis 11:1-9)? This "What if" is serious because when Nimrod and his followers decided to disobey God and not spread out across the globe God came down and mixed up their communication. This was the beginning of the earth having more than one language. That is not even the biggest aha moment in this story. On the day of Pentecost in Acts, in the second chapter, when the Holy Spirit first fell on the earth, all of a sudden all those gathered understood each other. That is because God caused those who spoke another language to speak the language of the person who heard them. For that moment in time, the languages were not confounded. This was a miraculous sign that the power of the Holy Spirit was at work. If Nimrod and his folks had never attempted to build a tower, this miraculous sign from heaven would not have been manifested forty-two generations later.

"What If" Joseph was never sold into slavery (Genesis 37:18-36)? The children of Israel would have all perished from starvation because when a famine came across the land Joseph would have still been living in Canaan with his family. Joseph's dream of ruling over his family would have had to come from another setting. The entire story of

Joseph found from Genesis 37 all the way to Genesis 50 would have been read an entirely different way. If Joseph's brothers had never been jealous of him and sold him into slavery he could not have interpreted the king's dream about corn and cows. The dream could not have made sense to anyone except one given the gift from God of dreaming and interpretation. That was Joseph and he had to be in Egypt where God would extend grace to feed the entire world during a famine. This "what if" could not have happened.

"What If" Moses did not accept the call from God to lead Israel out of Egypt? God cannot lie. He promised Abraham the land of Canaan. He also promised Abraham that He would make him a great nation with a seed that was as broad as the sands of the sea (Genesis 22:17). This could not have been fulfilled if the nation of Israel remained in slavery in Egypt. By the time God sent Moses to rescue them from Egyptian slavery, the king had begun to order that all the males of the Israelites be killed. That is a sure way to guarantee that an entire people be annihilated. The call to Moses was a personal one; these were his heritage of people he was being called to deliver. This is another dead "what if."

"What If," Joshua told Moses that he did not want to lead the Israelites into the Promised Land (Numbers 27:12-23)? Then just like the case with them in Egyptian slavery, all the Israelites would be dead. All two million of those in the wilderness would have died in the wilderness. Thank God that Joshua, even at an advanced age, had enough

17

mental fortitude and faith in God to continue the course that God designed when Moses led the Israelites out of slavery. Why would Joshua want to leave them in the wilderness? He would have also been killing his own reward of the Promised Land.

"What If" Deborah was not the first female judge (Judges 4-5)? You could not tell the story of Deborah being the first female judge of Israel. That is the simple answer. Not only was she the first judge, but God also gave her directions to tell the ruler of early Israel, Barak, to gather up the army and beat Jabin the king of Canaan. The reason Deborah's story is important is that her lead was based on spiritual authority. This was before Israel had its first king before they demanded to be just like the rest of the world. In this chapter in Judges, she was called the "mother in Israel" although she had no children. This is the level of respect given to her because they trusted her judgement. If she never became a judge, Barak may never have learned how to defeat the Canaanite army. It would just have been another cautionary tale of war and defeat. But, the fact that you are hearing about a great woman makes the story that much more interesting. This book is for everyone, but women listen to this fact: God used a woman to save a country. Without Deborah, no woman judge in the Bible with the accolade of being the Mother in Israel would have emerged.

"What If" Samson never told Delilah that his strength was in his hair locks (Judges 16)? For one, no one would hear how a woman used her feminine wows to get a man's secret. Although Sampson told his secret when he did not mean to, God still used him to win against the enemy. This happened after the enemy gouged out his eyes and cut his hair, thereby relieving him of his strength. God got the glory out of his life despite the fact that he had been swayed by the cunning of a woman. Divulging that his covenant to God as a Nazarite to never cut his hair, meant a loss of his superhuman strength, God surpassed all of that and extended Sampson's grace. This story of God's grace against the backdrop of human existence in a sinful world could never have been revealed had Sampson never told Delilah the secret of his strength.

"What If" Ruth took the advice of Naomi and went back to Moab (Ruth 1:16)? No one would ever have seen this story of sacrifice portrayed through love and loyalty being rewarded with greatness in the end than at the beginning of a young woman's life.

"What If" David did not kill Goliath (I Samuel 17:32-50)? This is a story of grace under fire. Even the king was afraid of the giant. David, before he was even king, showed that he knew where his courage came from. He was incensed that an enemy would defy the name of God. David, a mere child, destroyed a giant with a stone and a slingshot. If David had not killed Goliath his story would have taken on a different flavor. This story added to the powerful statement said about David that he was, "A man after God's own heart" (I Samuel 13:14). He was not at all perfect but had a heart for God's ways and it started from his younger days and continued throughout his reign as king.

The story of "what ifs" continue throughout the scripture. Suffice it to say that there are too many to count. The entire Bible is filled with steps of faith, miraculous rescues, healings, and decisions made with accurate wisdom. You want to align your life with examples of what can happen after a bad start, just open any chapter of the scripture.

Feel free, in addition to the ones already mentioned, to discover some of these stories from the scripture and do some comparison with your own seemingly insurmountable odds:

"What If" there was not a Prophet Elijah, "What If" Solomon prayed for long life, power, or money instead of God's Wisdom , "What If" Nehemiah did not build the wall, 'What If" Esther refused to go to the King, "What If" Job cursed God and died, "What If" Prophet Isaiah did not answer the Lord's call, 'I will go, Send me", "What If" Jeremiah told God to wait until he became an adult to speak to the people, "What If" Ezekiel did not prophesy to the dry bones, "What If" Daniel bowed down to King Nebuchadnezzar's golden image, "What If" Hosea did not marry an unfaithful woman, "What If" Joel never gave the prophecy about the Second Coming of Christ, "What If" Amos did not call the nation to repent, "What If" Obadiah did not pronounce judgment on other nations, "What If" Jonah was not thrown off the ship, "What If" Micah only prophesied doom, warning and despair, "What If" Nahum did not prophesied in the darkness of times to bring Hope, "What If" Habakkuk did not cry in anguish about the evil he was seeing around him, "What If" Zephaniah did not prophesize to tell the people to "Seek the Lord, all you humble of the land, you who do what He commands. Seek righteousness, seek humility, perhaps you will be sheltered on the day of the Lord's anger". Zephaniah 2:3, "What If" Haggai did not tell the people to rebuild the temple to bring back unity, faith, and strength, "What If" Zechariah did not prophesize about the coming of the Messiah, both his life and death and his future return to give the people full hope and encouragement, "What If" Malachi chose not to tell the people where they were falling short and in danger of hurting themselves and others again, "What If" the twelve Disciples decided not to follow Jesus and write the Gospels, "What If" Saul did not have the road to Damascus encounter, "What If", Peter did not preach to the Gentiles, "What If" John the Baptist did not want to preach Repentance and baptized people who received his message and "What If" God did not send His only begotten Son to die on the cross for our sins and then on the third day raise Him up with all Power in His Hand.

There were great people that God used to accomplish His will, purpose, and plan in the earth from the beginning of creation to the present time. However, God gives us a choice in every situation. Even Jesus had to come to Himself to choose God's will over His.

You will have to live out the consequences of your choices. You can choose to live out the reward of your obedience or suffer the consequences of following your own will. These are hard moments and the question always returns "what if". You are not given a "crystal ball" to see into your future; just remember the decisions that you make will influence your future.

The scriptures are filled with bad choices made by many people. You have examples to show you how to conduct your life. The next chapter will reveal some stories that can tell you what not to do and of course, there are the ones that tell you what to do when you make a wrong turn.

Chapter Three

COSTLY DECISIONS

No one has evaded all costly decisions. No one on earth makes the best choices all the time. Sometimes you may decide to act on your impulsiveness at the moment and then later realize that you simply "screwed up". Face the facts, everyone has made poor decisions at some time or another, perhaps the consequences were not as severe as others. Even though most people desire to always choose wisely, you will, at some point, stumble and fall.

I really believe that God left his Word to teach his way and to reveal examples of what happens when you do not. In the Bible, you can learn life lessons from Bible characters that made awful choices and then had to suffer the repercussions of those lapses in judgement.

Most Christians are aware of the story of Adam and Eve. Adam and Eve were warned by God not to eat the fruit from the Tree of Life. Eve listened to the snake who told her that she would not die but know good and evil like God. Eve ate from the fruit and then gave it to Adam who ate it too. God called out to Adam and Eve and both of them hid. God asked Adam, not Eve, why he ate of the tree. Adam responded that Eve, the woman God gave him, gave it to him and he did eat it. God then asked Eve why she ate from the tree. Eve's answer was like Adam's in that she casted blame. She told God that the serpent enticed her, and she ate it. From this first act of disobedience to God, sin, death, and suffering entered the entire world. It was at this point that God put Adam and Eve out of the beautiful place where they lived, the Garden of Eden.

There are scholars who believe that the serpent talked to Eve for more than one day to deceive her. However, Eve eventually decided to listen to the serpent and eat the fruit, not knowing that her sin of disobedience would cause all women thereafter to endure pain while giving birth. Women would also have the consequence of desiring to please their husbands while shrinking under the dominance of him having authority and being responsible for them. In addition to all of this, Adam would have to work hard all the days of his life while the earth would not cooperate and then return to the dust with Eve because of disobedience. To ask, "What If" Adam and Eve did not eat the fruit from the forbidden tree is useless. The fall of Adam and Eve was the plan of God from the beginning. However, the penalty for their act of disobedience, over 2,000 years later, is still in effect.

Esau was the firstborn of twins born to Isaac and Rebekah. His twin brother's name was Jacob. They were the grandsons of Abraham and Sarah. Esau is described in the Bible as a hunter, rough, tough, hairy, and a man of the field. Jacob stayed near their home and had a close relationship with his mother.

One day Esau had been in the field all day and returned home famished. Esau asked his younger brother for a bowl of the lentil stew he had cooking. Jacob offered Esau the stew in exchange for his birthright. In those days this was a big thing. According to Judaism, the firstborn was entitled to a double portion of his father's inheritance (Primogeniture - JewishEncyclopedia.com). Esau made the awful decision to exchange his inheritance and the position of leadership of the family for a bowl of soup. Was Esau that hungry that he could not eat leaves or berries or have a snack while preparing his own meal before giving Jacob his birthright? In those days there were no fast-food restaurants, but to sell your birthright for one meal could not have been a worse choice. Furthermore, it was not enough that Jacob had Esau's birthright, but with the help of his mother, the plot shifting continues. His mother overheard Isaac telling Esau that he was ready to pronounce the blessing over his life. Rebekah assisted Jacob in disguising himself as Esau in order to fool his now blind and elderly father to give him the firstborn's birthright blessing Jacob now becomes the spiritual leader of the family after Isaac's death and the heir of the promises of Abraham. Esau was furious and vowed to kill Jacob. In order to save Jacob from being killed by Esau, Rebekah tells Jacob to flee to a distant land and to work for his uncle Laban's household.

Esau's poor judgement resulted in the loss of inheritance and a distinct change in what was supposed to be his lifestyle as a family leader. "What If" Esau had his rightful place in his family and Abraham's blessings upon his life?

The story of Joseph is another example of one simple decision causing an upset in the family dynamics. Although Joseph was one of twelve sons he was his father's favorite being born later in his father's life. His father, Jacob, gave him a special coat of many colors which magnified Jacob's special love for him and brought out jealousy in his brothers. Joseph dreamed of ruling his family and decided to share this dream with his family. Unfortunately, this incident nearly cost Joseph his life since his brothers were already jealous of him. Reuben, the eldest of the brothers, convinced the rest of them not to kill him but to put him in a waterless pit. "What If" Joseph would have kept his mouth shut and never shared his dreams with his father and brothers until it came to pass? Joseph's decision to tell his family his dreams only made his brothers hate him more. His brothers knew that their father loved Joseph more than them; now Joseph is dreaming that they are bowing down before him too?

During the first time that Joseph was away from his father, the brothers were going to make it an opportunity to kill him. They believed they could become Joseph's worse nightmare and it would put to rest any chance of his dreams manifesting. Instead of killing him, his brother Judah suggests selling him to some of Ishmaelite's traders headed to Egypt. They then took his beautiful coat, covered it in animal blood, and told Jacob that Joseph had been torn to shreds by wild animals. Joseph was eventually sold into Egyptian slavery.

"What If" all of Joseph's brothers agreed to kill him? Joseph never would have been sold into slavery. But God always has a plan for your life even when you make wrong turns. Everything really does work out right according to what God has designed for your purpose.

Although Joseph shared his dream with his father and brothers he could not have known that his brothers would plot to kill him. The plan thwarted, Joseph later finds himself as a slave in the home of the captain of the army, Potiphar, where he finds favor. Joseph is given charge over everything in Potiphar's house. He trusted Joseph to make decisions regarding all of his business. Through many twists and turns, Joseph ends up in prison and eventually interpreting dreams for the King. His gift makes room for him and he ends up ruling Egypt where his family comes to get food when a deadly famine devastates the entire earth, His dream comes true; God's Will wins (story found in Genesis 37-50).

Because of the famine on the earth, all of Joseph's family ends up coming to Egypt. Just as God had promised to Abraham, his seed is multiplying (Genesis 22:17), and soon the Hebrews are outnumbering the Egyptians. Pharaoh, the name for the king in Egypt, desiring to maintain balance and control, makes the Hebrews slaves. This Pharaoh has come years after Joseph and has no clue of his leadership. But God is about to send help. The book of Exodus tells of the miraculous rescue of the Hebrews from Egyptian slavery. He used Moses, a Hebrew who had been raised in the king's house as a prince. But, it would not at all be an easy task. It would take ten plagues, the final one being the death of the firstborn child before God would soften the heart of Pharaoh to allow the children to be led by Moses into the wilderness and away from Egypt.

Moses led God's chosen people out of the land of Egypt, into the wilderness, and in the direction that God leads towards a promised land. During the journey, the Hebrews became impatient with their circumstances and the journey would last forty years instead of a couple of weeks. Moses missed out on the opportunity to enter the Promised Land because he did not as God put it, "honor me as holy in the sight of the Israelites, you will not bring this community into the land I give them" (Numbers 20:12). All God told him to do was to hit a rock that would bring forth water for the thirsty people. Angry with all of their complaining, Moses hit the rock twice and brought attention to his actions rather than God's miracle. Moses's leadership was over at the entrance to the Promised Land.

This next story gives you another great theme woven throughout scripture, God does not love you according to how perfect you are, but according to how much your heart is toward him. The second king of Israel was King David who lusted after the wife of one of his soldiers, Bathsheba the wife of Uriah was bathing on the top of her roof while her husband was off at war. King David saw her and immediately began his plot to get what his flesh desired. He ended up sleeping with Bathsheba, impregnating her, and then setting up Uriah to seem like he was the father. Unwilling to leave the battlefield, King David has Uriah killed in battle and takes Bathsheba as his wife. Through his tears and repentance, God still allowed David's firstborn to become ill and die. All of this yet God continued his plan of letting Jesus come through the family line of David.

Ending this chapter is the best example of wrong decisions leading to the fulfillment of God's ultimate plan. Judas Iscariot was one of Jesus's original Twelve Apostles. Jesus knew, from the foundation of the world, that Judas was going to betray Him for 30 pieces of silver. Judas brought the men to arrest Jesus and identified him with a kiss. Jesus was then arrested, put on trial, and crucified. Judas's decision cost him his life. Judas committed suicide.

Everyone has made decisions in a moment that caused much suffering and pain. These decisions impacted your lives and changed your world forever. When a woman is informed by her doctor that she is pregnant, she has to choose to give birth, put the baby up for adoption or have an abortion. For some women the choices are hard and for other women, the choices are easy.

I was a single mom at age 27 and went on to have my second child at age 30 while still not being married. I chose to have my babies and raise them as a single parent. I have met women who decided to make the choice to place their child up for adoption and then later wonder what kind of life the child has. I have met women who had an abortion or several abortions and wonder "What If" I did not kill my child, what was the sex of the baby, how would the child look, what would the child have become in life, and other questions that they will never know.

Most people struggle with costly decisions because choosing one alternative means giving up another. People can sometimes be haunted by their decisions because they really do not know if they made the best choice. One of the best ways to make better decisions is to have what is called an informed decision. These are decisions made with all the information you can gather concerning the matter before finalizing the choice. Second, you have to listen to that quiet spirit inside you and obey. I have two personal experiences that ended up being very costly because I did not listen or obey that voice in my spirit that told me to play the lottery.

In 1994, I played the New York Lottery after consistent encouragement from my mother. I had never played the lottery in my life. My conviction at that time as a Christian was that Believers didn't gamble. Gambling was a sin. I allowed religion to trick me. However, I decided to play, I literally felt unction to play. It is a feeling that is indescribable. The exact 6 numbers just came to my mind. I placed 3 in the first box and 3 in the second box. My brother, who was going to the store to play our lottery tickets for my mother and I, glanced at the card and told me that I completed it wrong. I heard that still voice say, "Regina, put the same exact numbers in the second box and in the first box with the other three". I ignored that voice and asked my nieces and nephews, who were visiting with their grandmother, for their favorite numbers which I used to complete the lottery card. Even when I left my mother's house with my daughter to return home, I felt like I should fill out another card with the initial first six numbers. However, my religious beliefs said, "You cannot stand on a lottery line to purchase tickets; "What If" your church friends see you?" My pride and religious beliefs would not allow me to go play the lottery. Later that evening, the 10 pm News came on and the reporter was at a store doing a story on how the lines were still long with people vying for a chance to win the 72 Million dollar Lottery jackpot. The ticket sales would cease at 10:45 PM. At that time, the lottery jackpot was the largest in New York history. I still had this strong unction to go play those initial six numbers, but I thought again about the chance of my unsaved friends seeing me stand in the lottery line. I just knew that would be a poor witness. I talked myself out of it again. At 10:15 pm, I refer to this moment as my final call, something inside me said, get my daughter up who was in her crib asleep and go play the lottery. I still did not listen, making all the excuses up in the world. The next morning, my brother heard the announcement of the winning number and told my mother that he remembered me having those numbers on the ticket that I gave him. My mother called me to check the ticket that my brother took to the store for me and there it was the six initial numbers on the ticket but 3 in the first box and three in the second box not in the same roll. I felt a pang in the pit of my stomach. I really could have won the lottery What if I listened to that small inner voice, What if I had been obedient, What if I did not let man's religious traditions get the best of me, and What If I became a Millionaire. I let an uninformed decision cost me dearly. The moment slipped away from me. Four people in New York shared that Jackpot.

Three years later, after moving to Ohio, I had a similar moment as I had in New York. That morning I literally got off my knees from praying and six numbers came to my mind. I wrote them down and had that same feeling that had come to me three years earlier. That inner voice told me to take that piece of paper with me to work and to play the lottery during my lunch hour. Did I do it? No! I told myself that I would play them later. At the time I did not even know how much the Ohio Super Lotto Jackpot of 1997 was. At work, my co-workers were talking about the lottery jackpot being 30 million dollars since no one had won the previous drawing. Then I remembered that I had left the numbers at home on my coffee table. After work, I gathered my children from the babysitter and childcare facility then headed home. My aunt phoned me and at the end of the conversation, she said that she was going to the store to play her numbers and I recalled again the Jackpot is 30 million dollars. I started to ask her if she could play the numbers for me, then I changed my mind considering that she might want to share in my winnings. The chance of me winning felt really possible with what had taken place in New York.

What if I win and my aunt did not tell me, What If she says that she didn't play it or forgot to play it, What if she says, "Well you did not give me the money so it is my ticket". To avoid any of the above, I said that I would just play it after dinner. It was now close to 7 pm and I had a few minutes to go across the street and play the six numbers for the Ohio lottery Jackpot, but I allowed excuses to come into play again. One of my daughters had fallen to sleep already; I would have to wake her up. I did not want to leave them in the car and I did not have anyone to watch them. I definitely did not want to stand in a long line with them. Ultimately, these thoughts had nothing to do with my daughters. They were excuses; just like I had previously.

I was tired and did not want to go back outside with my children. Some single parents can understand that after working a long day, picking up children from two different locations, going home to cook, feeding the kids, trying to get their bath; the thought of putting shoes and jackets back on, getting them into the car seats is just too tiring! Sometimes as a single parent after a long stressful day at work, you just want to finish up mommy duties and get your kids in bed so you can wind down. In addition, at that time I was living in a two-bedroom apartment complex, so I saw it as a hassle to go back outside again. I would have to put my children back in my van only to stand-in, perhaps, a long line at the Big Bears grocery store. For a quick moment, I wrestled with myself thinking of a plan B. Maybe I could put them both in the crib and run to the store. However, I could not see leaving my children at home alone. What if something happened to them while I was gone, What if they climbed out the crib and opened the door or set a fire, and then I would go to jail because I was at the store playing the lottery. That was not an option anymore. All these thoughts made me even more tired and reluctant. I did not go.

Literally at 7:40 pm, I was in the bathroom when I heard from speakers of the television set in the living room the Official Lottery Officer call the winning numbers out for the Super Lotto. I ran to the coffee table and could not believe that all six numbers were on that little piece of paper! It seemed unbelievable. History was repeating itself. How could I ignore that inner voice again! The "What ifs" began to play in my mind! The next day, the local News Reporter announced no-one had won the Jackpot! What If, I had played the numbers on my lunch break, What If I gave my aunt the numbers to play, What if I just took my kids with me to the store, or What If I left them alone at home for a few minutes to play the Lotto? It was just another moment of a missed opportunity and I was left to deal with the costly consequences for my indecision!

How did I let two opportunities pass me by? Will there ever be another chance to win the lottery? Why did not I apply the lessons learned from disobedience and pride from the first situation and let them be my guide? I thought a few times over the years how my life and family's life would have been different with those lottery winnings, what house I would have purchased for my family. Would I have moved from New York to a region that is sunny and warm every day, what opportunities would I have given my children? Would I have raised them differently? Would it have been better or would they have been totally spoiled and privileged? My kids *would* have had a different

34

childhood. I would have exposed them to the world and traveled to lavish adventures. They would have had their college expenses paid in full with no student loans needed. They would have had money to invest in their own businesses. Over the years the "What Ifs" rang loud in my head.

On the other hand, I think of all the wonderful co-workers and friends that I now have who I probably would have never met at work or church or in the two neighborhoods where I have lived. I have life-long friends that are priceless and certainly mean more to me than money. My close friends are like family. What if I never met them because our paths would not have crossed if I was retired at age 28 or 31 years old if I won the New York or Ohio lottery?

The lessons that I learned in both situations above would not have been allowed in the religious circles where I was taught or from any other religious people who seek to dictate the lives of fellow believers. The only right way is to know God's word and to follow the leading of the Holy Spirit. You must listen and obey His voice. God will lead and guide you every step of the way and assist you in getting rid of pride that blocks you from embracing the truth. God has blessed my "alternative" life situation in spite of not winning a lump sum of money in the lottery. My life is blessed. I am happy and learned to be content in every aspect of my life. Honestly, I cannot see a different life than the one I have lived, past and present. However, lessons learned; I won't miss another opportunity to play the lottery again if I ever get that unexplainable unction to play! My sister in Christ, who lives in New York, listened to the spirit several years ago and acted on that unction to purchase a Scratch-off at the grocery store where she once worked. She won $1,000,000. Listen, "Maybe God isTryin To Tell You Somethin" song by Quincy Jones.

Chapter Four

DEFINING MOMENTS IN AMERICAN HISTORY

I want to challenge you to use your imagination and think about the world differently. What if some of the history-changing decisions made by some men and women in the United States were not made? These decisions were made by former presidents, community activists, and other leaders.

Think about some of the incidences from history. We all should know by now that Christopher Columbus did not discover America. What would America look like today if the Native Americans were not removed from their ancestral lands, tribes, and able to maintain their hunting grounds and agricultural ways and not forced into one-sided treaties and discriminatory governing policies? What would Africa look like today if Africans were able to live on their land, build their own cities, trade, and have their own culture, religion, and traditions? Can you imagine if Harriet Tubman decided not to be the conductor on the Underground Railroad? She led enslaved people to freedom before the Civil War. Some of you never learned any of this in history while others heard the contrived versions.

What if Rosa Parks elected to give up her seat to the white man on the bus? The Tulsa Race Massacre started with the false reporting of an incident that happened in an elevator between a black shoe shine man, Dick Rowland, and a white woman Sarah Page, the elevator operator. No one knows exactly what happened, but Mr. Rowland seemingly was involved in a small physical incident with Ms. Page (What is 'Black Wall Street? History of the community and its massacre (cnbc.com). He either bumped into her or possibly stepped on her foot. Ms. Page screamed, which was not an unusual occurrence during the early 1900s when white women closely encountered black men and racial tension was on the rise throughout the country. Someone who heard the scream called the police and Mr. Rowland was arrested. The Tulsa Tribune falsely reported that Mr. Rowland had assaulted Ms. Page (rumors even spread that he had raped her) and a riot ensued that took the lives of nearly 300 black people. This happened near the Greenwood District of Tulsa, Oklahoma. This was a community of rich black people where they had established a self-contained neighborhood that included a hospital. Black Wall Street in Oklahoma's Greenwood District could have paved the way as an example to other black communities in developing their own luxury shops, restaurants, movie theaters, libraries, pool halls, and nightclubs. Ms. Park's actions started the early movements toward civil rights and the Tulsa situation opened the eyes of black people to what could be done collectively, even with all the persecutions by those that thought otherwise.

What if Dr. Martin Luther King, Jr. refused to lead the civil rights movement? What if Malcolm X did not go to Mecca? What if Barack Obama opted out of the presidency? What If Oprah Winfrey never had a nationally syndicated talk show? What if Tyler Perry listened to his critics? All of these occurrences are forever etched in black history and make an impression on the consciousness of many blacks.

What if the four men from the terrorist group Al-Qaeda did not board those planes that attacked America on September 11, 2001? What if the Continental Congress did not approve the Declaration of Independence? What if President Abraham Lincoln decided not to issue the Emancipation Proclamation? What If the good folks at the NAACP and Thurgood Marshall did not take up their case ultimately called Brown vs. Board of Education? What if President John F. Kennedy was not assassinated? What if NASA Staff did not send the Space Shuttle to the moon and there was no Apollo 11 mission? What if the Supreme Court did not pass the Roe v. Wade law? What if the women involved in the women's rights and suffrage movements stayed home and chose not to fight for women to be involved in the political process or have equal rights? What if William J. Seymour had made the decision not to follow God's leading to start the Azusa Street Revival? From life's disruptions to the regeneration of spirits, some decisions have far-reaching consequences.

All the above decisions made by men and women shaped the American culture and history. Each one impacted and affected our world. There are no alternatives for the things that happened in the past. All of them happened and you must remember them to do better, live better, make adjustments, change if necessary, and accept the truth.

I am a black woman born in America in the '60s, not Africa. I thank God that I was not born during slavery. I am certain that I would have been killed the moment I was able to say, "No" and "Stop" to a slave owner. God allowed my existence to begin on February 7, 1966. I am convinced that I was born when I was supposed to for Such a Time as This! I do not know when God will transition me from this world to my eternal home. However, I do not want to miss the plan of God for my life. I do not want my living on this planet to be in vain. I am working on the dash that will be displayed on my obituary one day: 1966 -. You all must make decisions with the time you have between your life and death. What will be your legacy? How will you be remembered? What did you teach the next generation? Who did you disciple? What inheritance will you leave your grandbabies, who I would like to refer to as grand-gifts? Your decisions are your own. However, the choices you make can impact others. You cannot go back and change what was, but you can make more informed decisions now.

One pivotal moment in my history changed my life forever. It was solely based on my mother's decision to not renew her apartment lease. I grew up in a single-family home in the projects in Hempstead, New York. The area has now been named "Mid-way" because it is located between the heights and the hills in my town. My mother, older brother, and I resided in this low-income townhouse apartment complex. I have fond childhood memories of playing with my peers, walking to school, getting into mischief, and learning how to survive the stereotypical poor black community mentality. One day my father comes to visit and tells my mother that he purchased a house in an affordable neighborhood and wants his family to move out of the projects to "his dream home". He had come to rescue us and give us a better quality of life.

The offer from my father sounded good but I did not want to leave my comfort zone. I had resided in that two-bedroom apartment from age 6-14 years old. I was established, secure, knew the people in my village, and frankly did not want to leave my residence. In addition, I felt that my parents were once again in the "honeymoon stage" of their marriage. I believed the cycle of abuse would resume once the honeymoon stage ended. I just knew the chaos would start over again and was I concerned about how that would affect my brother and I.

My mother made the awful decision to pack up our lives and move to the "promise land"/my father's house in Roosevelt, New York. Less than three months later, the honeymoon period was over between my parents, and my father was kicking us out of his house. He accused my mother's sister, who was residing with us at the time, of throwing away his important retirement papers. Although, I was shocked, I was not surprised because I had lived most

41

of my life experiencing my parent's heated and volatile relationship, triggered by trivial matters. But this made no sense that my biological father was putting his children and wife out on the streets for a mistake that my Aunt made? The hopes of a different ending were short-lived.

The next day, my mother, brother and I were heading to my mother's other sister's home to take up temporary residence with her, her husband, and six children in a three-bedroom house in Freeport, New York. Throughout all of these moves, all over Long Island, I remained enrolled in the Hempstead school district. I commuted from both places to the Hempstead School district. I am not sure how this took place, but I can only surmise that no one ever transferred my records from Hempstead to the location of my father's home then my Aunt's house. God kept me under the radar and I didn't have to switch schools at any time. After a brief stay at my aunt's home, I felt the tension commonly known as, "You have worn out your welcome and it is time for you to go!" Therefore, under duress, my mother signed a rental lease agreement to move back into an apartment in Hempstead.

I am now feeling secure again; we finally have our own place. Although it was in a high crime area it was ours, a place to call "home sweet home". I could survive the neighborhood fights, crime, and violence because I had experience from my previous stay in the projects. I knew to mind my business, stay quiet and keep walking until I made it into the apartment. Less than a year later, living in this same apartment, my mother comes home from work and announces with a stoic face, "I had to find a place to live". At this time my brother was not living with us. My mother informed me that she would not be renewing the lease and that *I* needed to ask a family at my local church if I could live with them. I was attending a church that my older sister, Michele Hollingsworth, had invited me to when I was twelve; she would come to pick me up for services. She was one sibling from my mother's first marriage. Thank God for this ministry, but this was the worst way that a mother could destroy the security of an adolescent.

At this time I am fifteen years old. It felt like I had been soccer punched; here was another nightmare. For one I was shocked, and you can only imagine all the other emotions that I had at the time. Coming from my own mother, this could not have been worse. A mother, whom a child expects to protect her, keep her safe, love and nurture her, is now telling her teenage daughter to make her own living arrangements. After this pronouncement, she is now directing me to speak with a family that I really had no close relationship with, and ask them to take me in. To top it off, my mother did not even attend this church. I honestly felt like an orphan, a motherless child! I now felt abandoned by both parents! This was not love. I asked my mother where she was going to live, and she responded that she was going to stay in a room in a friend's home and that there was no room for me. Then she just walks away.

I remember standing in the apartment in disbelief. It was the Word of God at that moment that grabbed hold of my spirit and said; "When your mother and father forsake you, I will lift you up" (Psalm 27:11 KJV). I did not know how God was going to shelter me, but I had to trust him and his plan for my life in this season! This was in the '80s and I did not have a cell phone or even a house phone for that matter. My shock and disbelief had to immediately translate into action.

My relatives in New York were not able to provide shelter for me and besides that, I had not been in contact with them. One aunt had already kicked us out of her place, and my older siblings, from my mother's first marriage, were living their lives. Frankly, I did not know how or if I wanted to contact them. Remember, I am fifteen and having to make a decision that no teenager should have to make. As a teenager, I was facing homelessness in America and it seemed like my only option was to go into a shelter. I did not even know where the shelters were and I wondered what would happen to my personal belongings and schooling. I was in high school, highly active, and doing well! I was not aware of Child Protective Services or who to talk to about housing arrangements. All I knew was that I did not want to go into the Foster Care system. Where was I going to get help?

Just for a moment, I need to take you back to my childhood apartment complex where I lived from the age of 6-14. This is the place where I was at peace and content living with my mother and brother. This was before we moved in with my father to what was presented as his "dream home". At this time I was about seven years old when a new family moved into the townhouse next door to us. They were a young couple with a son around three years old. I was excited to play with their son. I felt like his "big sister" and I would watch him ride his tricycle on the pavement in front of the apartment building. I recall him being full of energy with a big 1970's afro. I remember the wife chatting with my mother and getting advice; she was always respectful towards my mom. These times hold a special place in my memory. They were the best of times.

I recall about a year later, the family packing up and saying bye to us. They were relocating to another apartment building managed by the same management company as the complex where we lived. My mother had encouraged them to apply for the new place because the wife had become pregnant with their second child and the family needed a larger apartment unit. I was so sad to see the friendly neighbors leave with my "little brother". I never saw the family again until years later after my oldest sister, Michele Hollingsworth, who was attending Refuge Church of Christ in Freeport, NY, asked me to babysit my nephew and a few of her choir friends' children while they had a group date night with their husbands. I was thirteen years old and about to babysit for at least six children ages ranging from 4 years old to 10 years old. I agreed, and one of the choir members, Romona Phillips walked into my sister's home with her two children and looked at me, and said, "I know you". She then turned to my sister, Michele, and continued to tell me how she knew me. Turns out, this was the mother that used to live next door to us. She was totally unaware that I was Michele's little sister. She probably had not noticed me before now because I was not in her circle of friends at church since I was so young. We had not seen each other in over six years since she moved from the apartment next door to ours.

Romona got her son's attention and then asked me if I remembered him. Romona's son, Shawndu, was now nine years old, no longer riding a tricycle, and was now much taller. Then Romona introduced me to her daughter, Teishia, the one with who Romona was pregnant when the family moved to a different apartment complex. This was divine intervention, a pivotal moment that would prove to change my life forever. Those six years probably seemed much longer to a three year old child, but they would be the timing God needed to put a plan in action.

Let's go back to where I left off with my mother's announcement that I would have to exit the apartment in two weeks. What was a 15 year old girl supposed to do when the only parent providing her basic necessities tells her to find her own housing because the parent is not renewing the lease where she lived? She claimed that the rent was not affordable anymore, and to make it more unfathomable, she had already made arrangements for her own provision that did not include me. In addition, this mother asks her child to fend for herself by asking "someone" at church to provide housing for her.

By now my sister Michele had left the church where she witnessed and shared the good news of the Gospel of Jesus Christ with me. It was then that I accepted Jesus as my Lord and Savior and became a member of the church where my sister and Romona sang in the choir together, fellowshipped, and worshipped. I had found other transportation to and from church. My mother did not attend the church because her faith was Baptist and my father did not attend the Pentecostal Apostolic Holiness church because he claimed to be a Muslim.

After my sister left the church, I thought about leaving too. It was Michele that introduced me to God, transported me to and from the house of worship, and/or made arrangements for my rides to the church on days she would not be attending. She purchased for me the required church attire, choir uniforms, and robes for my participation. My older sister was nine years older than me; she was my role model and a second mother to me. She shared with me why she was leaving the church and told me that it would be my decision if I too wanted to leave. However, I did not want to base my decision on her experience, so I chose to stay. I had already developed friendships with my peers and my church had become my spiritual family. In addition, it was an easy decision for me to continue at the local church because we had the absolute best youth leader in our Dioceses.

Delores Rickenbacker, who we affectionately called Cook or Cookie, was the Youth Leader. Cookie encouraged me to stay connected to the ministry, remain actively involved in the youth group, and develop a personal relationship with Christ by praying, fasting, and reading the Bible. Cookie was invested in all the lives of the young people at the church. She made serving God fun by providing outings and activities for us throughout the year. Cook organized enjoyable events and entertainment at church, after church, and on the weekends. Cook's home was a haven for the young people. We had the liberties to be ourselves, laugh, and talk to Cook about any and everything.

At an early age, Cook made us entrepreneurs. She would give us boxes of candy to sell to raise money to travel with our Pastor to National Conventions and Conferences. She included everyone. She would support us at our school events by bringing the entire youth group to the activity. I will never forget how she surprisingly brought the entire youth group to my high school senior's award night and how they cheered for me after every announcement for an award I received, screaming my church's nickname, "Bouche, Bouche, Bouche"! They were the loudest crowd in the audience. Cook and my church family had become my family by love after my blood family disappeared out of my life for the season that my parents forsook and abandoned me! Besides entrepreneur skills, I learned the dynamics of a real family.

It was Cook that took approximately six graduates from the Class of 1984 to New York City for a dinner and to see the Off-Broadway play, 'Mama I want to Sing' starring Desiree Coleman. Cook told us to dress up because she was taking us out for a memorable evening since the young people were discouraged by the church organization, at that time, from attending the prom which they called "worldly".

Cookie gave us a remarkable senior night that we all enjoyed.

Cook made serving God gratifying. The young people did not have to smoke cigarettes or marijuana or drink or go to clubs to have a good time. We wanted to chase after God and pursue His Kingdom. Honestly, I did not feel that I was missing out on worldly things or events because I was young, saved, and being taught how to enjoy this godly life. Cook was my friend, mentor, cheerleader, role model, and sister in Christ. Ultimately, if Cook were not in my life when my sister left Refuge church, I would have left the church too and missed out on what would become one of the greatest blessings in my life.

Cook was also known for making us her famous Jello cake! Later, Cook and her family relocated to Georgia and that was the state where Cookie transitioned from this life to receive her eternal reward in January 2017. My sister, Michele, went to another assembly where she accepted her call to preach the Gospel and that is where she was attending when she passed away in June 1996. These were two of the best people in my life, gone twenty-one years apart.

I believe that God orchestrates our lives, nothing happens by chance. One of my closest friends in the youth group was Cookie's first cousin, Marion. She and I lived in the same town when my mother gave me the eviction notice. I was 15 years old with nowhere to go. Marion was 18 years old living with her parents. I had two bags of belongings and no money. I asked Marion if I could stay the night over her house. That one night turned into almost a week. Then Marion asked me if I had housing. I finally shared with Marion that I had no shelter and was trying to figure out where I was going next. During my unexpected stay at Marion's parent's apartment, her mother willingly provided me with food, drink, and a place to lay my head. I am thankful that her parents opened their hearts and home to me. God really does know how to provide. This was definitely not a coincidence. God was up to something.

One morning Marion left the apartment while I was asleep and came back to inform me that she had spoken with Romona and Romona wanted to meet with me. You remember Romona, she was my sister's friend at church and the lady that used to live next door to me in the townhouse.

I recall being nervous, especially since Marion stated that Romona wanted to meet with me alone. I literally had no clue what she wanted to talk to me about. Marion simply gave me Romona's address and then said that she and I would talk when I returned. I went to Romona's home and she asked me to have a seat at the kitchen table. Romona began to explain to me that Marion had informed her of my housing situation and that she had spoken to her husband, Fite. She wanted to offer me a place to live! At that moment, Romona reminded me that it was my mother who, six years earlier, had aided her family in obtaining that larger apartment when she was pregnant with her baby, Teishia. Romona shared that my mother was kind to her family, she knew my sister who had once attended church with her, and now she wanted to bless me by offering me housing. Now, here is a family I met when I was seven years old, did not see them again until I was thirteen years old and at age fifteen, I would be living with them. Only God knew that I would live with them throughout my high school journey and undergraduate college years!

There is so much I can share regarding my experience of becoming a family member in the Phillips home. However, I will share a few life-changing experiences that have impacted my life forever!!!

I learned that love is unconditional and does not keep a record of wrongdoings. My mother agreed to pay the Phillips twenty dollars a week for my food. Romona stated that she was not going to charge my mother a fee for rent since I would be sharing the bedroom with her daughter. My mother paid the family three times during my initial stay. The last two times we hunted her down and found her at a gambling table. After my mother avoided us for the fourth time and had her friend tell Romona that she was not in the house while she was there playing cards, Romona said that she would never again chase my mother down for twenty dollars. She told me that I was now part of the family and I should never feel unworthy to eat with them because my mother had not contributed for the food. I told Romona that I would get a job during the school year to help financially. After all, I had worked every summer since I was thirteen years old and had been responsible for purchasing my own school clothes. Her response to me was that the greatest gift I could give her and Fite was completing my education and obtaining my high school diploma. She gave me permission to continue working only during the summer months. It was such godly love she and her family showed to me.

Not only did I gift them with a high school diploma, I, by the grace of God exceeded their expectations and I graduated from high school with honors in three years and was offered a full scholarship to Hofstra University under the auspicious of the NOAH (New Opportunities at Hofstra) program in Hempstead, New York. Later, I continued my education at Fordham University Lincoln Center in New York where I received my master's degree in Social Work.

Living with the Phillips family, I began to value family, positions, and roles. I developed new traditions. I learned to corporately participate in household chores and follow household rules and expectations. I learned to value hard work and education. I learned to prioritize, set goals and pursue them. Romona and Fite had become second parents to me and my support system. Shawndu and Teishia were now my little brother and sister and I felt obligated to set a good example for them. I had a family who believed in me. We watched movies together, laughed together, talked to each other, and attended church together. Now I know what a family looks like. We were not perfect, but we had each other's backs and respect for one another! God allowed me to live in the Phillips' home to experience an environment cultivated by unconditional love, peace, celebrations, and non-violence! Romona was a mother-figure, friend, confidant, and sister in the Lord! Fite was the provider, protector, and on the weekends cooked the best breakfasts. On Thursday nights, his payday, he treated the family to McDonalds, and on Saturday mornings he made the best pancakes in the world! We had so much fun, fond memories, and laughs on Elm Ave. in Hempstead. After all this time we still enjoy laughable moments when one word or phrase is spoken that reminds us of those old days. The Phillips family knows that they will always be a part of my life, Romona transitioned to her eternal rest in October 2018.

Everyone's life has a story with twists and turns. Your past is a part of your history, filled with defining moments, pleasant and unpleasant. Some decisions in your past were made by other people that you had no control over, and those choices affected your lives positively or negatively. Even you made decisions that chartered the course of your life and had to pay the repercussions or reap the rewards.

What if the Phillips family never moved next door to us? What if my mother never moved away from the projects? What if my sister had never attended "that" church? What if Cook was not the youth leader? What if Marion and I were never close friends? What if I was placed in foster care? What if I had to live in a homeless shelter? What if I had to drop out of high school to work? What if my father provided for his family? What if a relative was able to offer me a place to stay?

You cannot change the past or undo it. There are past hurts and wounds that you endured because of the choices someone else made for you. I have an older friend born in the 1950's whose foster mother's son-in-law sexually abused her from ages 15 to 17 years old then kicked her out of the house when she became pregnant with his baby during her senior year in high school. They said they were "protecting" their family. The foster parent forced my friend to tell the principal at school that she was pregnant and the principal's response was to immediately unenroll her from the district. In one day, she was homeless and deprived of an education. The staff at the school contacted her uncle and his wife to make arrangements for her to live with them. How do you tell your child that they are a product of the mother being sexually abused and the product of an unwanted pregnancy? Unfortunately, there are millions of young boys and girls that were raped, sexually abused, and molested by strangers, trusted neighbors, family members, schoolteachers, preachers, Boy Scout leaders, coaches, and other sexual predators. There are people that are physically abused by someone who chose not to control their anger and strike them out of rage. Some people have experienced verbal, mental and emotional abuse. These things happened, but unfortunately cannot be undone.

There are fathers and husbands who decided to leave home and their responsibilities. There are parents that make the decision to abandon their children for numerous selfish reasons: drugs, alcohol, a relationship, career, or for a different lifestyle without. There are mentally ill individuals who choose not to take their medications and as a result, spend most of their life in a mental health facility. There are people who choose not to take prescription medications from their doctor and/or choose an alternative route. There are many disruptions to the wholesome family setting.

Case after case, scenarios after scenarios, and situations after situations, consequences, and rewards or decisions have been made that had an impact on the trajectory of your life. You have made choices that sent you down a path that formed a future you did not imagine. Furthermore, there are times when people are not aware that an emotion, thought or reaction is coming from a past experience, a level of pain, or a traumatic event, and others are impacted by your responses and reactions. This next chapter will reveal how other decisions coupled with actions can alter the direction of your life.

I would be remiss to not share with you before ending this chapter, for inquiring minds, that my biological father died in February 1993 in Cleveland, Ohio at age 58. There was a time before his death, he and I resolved to not debate over religion. There were several times that he asked me "to pray to my God" for him! I remember having wonderful Christmas and birthday gifts from my father before my "Born Again" experience. When I was in second grade, my father purchased a typewriter and told me to learn how to type because I was not going to be somebody's homemaker! I admired my father's beautiful penmanship and outgoing and charismatic personality. He introduced me to Jazz music at an early age. My father was a community activist; instrumental in obtaining signatures to petition the courts to make Martin Luther King Jr.'s Birthday a Federal Holiday. In addition, he volunteered at a local CETA-(Comprehensive Employment and Training Act) program to help young people gain employment in the 1970s. He was called, "Black Moses" in the community and also Isaac Hayes because he favored him. My father retired as a supervisor from the Department of Sanitation at age 55.

God restored my relationship with my biological mother after undergraduate school. She is currently in my life, loved by her family and she has been a blessing to us throughout the years!

And my friend who chose to give birth against all odds, her son is a powerful preacher and pastor today! What if she aborted his destiny? At the age 19, she continued her education and obtained her G.E.D. and afterwards a college degree.

Chapter Five

RELATIONSHIPS (HE LOVES ME, HE LOVES ME NOT)

The Song of Solomon is a romantic book that depicts people in love in the Bible. It is written as one continuous poem. This book in the Bible should be enjoyed by intimate lovers of any age. The Song of Solomon has been said to also reflect the love of Christ for his bride, which is the church.

There are many who highlights all of the sexual entanglements that culminate in dangerous and sinful relationships. The Bible does give us examples of people who fell in love with the wrong person or inappropriately engaged in sexual encounters. Of course, there is Samson and Delilah, the Samaritan woman at the well, to the adulterous woman who was brought to Jesus because she was caught in the act of adultery. I believe that Solomon's poetry found in the Bible Book the Song of Solomon helps to offset the sinful acts of the world. It stands to show that romantic passion is a great thing between lovers in the institution of marriage.

Solomon's poem begins with two lovers in courtship. They express how much they love each other and their fiery desire for affection. In the end, they come together in marriage, the groom praising his bride's beauty. The bride struggles with the thought that her husband may abandon her, while the groom promises always to be faithful. Ultimately, all the poetic words are examples of the expressions said by lovers longing to be in love and married to each other.

Most women want a man that loves her as Christ loved the church so much that he gave his life for His bride. Most women want the affection, affirmation, and praise of their lover. Most women want a man to protect and provide for them. Most women are ready for love, to become a wife and mother. Most women want the fairy tale story at the end. Most men want a wife that they can trust, rely upon, and build a dynasty with. Most humans want someone that they are physically attracted to. Most people will at least one time in their life experience love and "be" in love. I have met people of all ages who said that they are still waiting to find their soul mate, someone with who they connect emotionally, mentally, spiritually, and physically.

You have to make choices and decisions when it comes to your mates. Dating is a process. Dating gives you the opportunity to gather data on an individual to help you decide if that person is compatible with you. You want to know if that person is a good fit in your lifestyle and will blend with your future goals. Let's face the fact most of you have a checklist of what you want in a relationship. While dating, you are either checking items off the list that the person meets or nodding your head saying, "No he or she is not the one." Most people make their checklist based upon their personal desires, religious beliefs, values, standards, and expectations.

I want to help my single brothers and sisters in the Body of Christ when it comes to Biblical views on dating and/or marrying someone. Consider the following scriptures: II Corinthians 6:14 reads in the Amplified Bible, "Do not be unequally bound together with unbelievers [do not make mismatched alliances with them, inconsistent with your faith]. For what partnership can righteousness have with lawlessness? Or what fellowship can light have with darkness?" Who is an unbeliever? An unbeliever is someone who does not believe in Jesus Christ; represents everything opposed to the Christian faith and someone who has not allowed Jesus to be Lord of his or her life.

In addition, Amos 3:3 (KJV) reads, "Can two walk together, except they be agreed?" I encourage you to make a list of how many things you actually agree upon. Discover as many topics in the universe that means the most to you to determine if you two are "on the same page" regarding issues and things that matter to you. You do not want to marry someone who is not in agreement with your matters of the heart. I firmly believe that society has told believers to make these long lavish checklists in choosing a mate, but the Bible only requires two: not to marry an unbeliever and to get someone that you have more things that agree on than disagree with.

The Bible is so simple but sometimes it is presented as being complex. There are two Kingdoms in this world. God has a Kingdom and the world has a kingdom. Simply put,

God's Kingdom for believers is doing things God's way instead of the world system/society's way. In other words, God has left his Word-His last Will and Testament for the church. As a Christian your actions should be living and doing things God's way according to His Kingdom. God never told you to make a list and write down what you want in a mate. The world system told you to make a list because in their system most of the things on the checklist come from their picture of success. It says you should look for a mate with a college degree, a matching or exceeding income, a good credit score, and no kids from a previous relationship. This is the man-made worldly way of looking for a mate. So many sisters and brothers have walked away from good women and men in the church because of these unrealistic checklists and they have operated in the world's way of thinking rather than the Kingdom of God.

What If you would have given that person without a college degree a chance? What If you would have dated that blue-collar worker? What if you looked at the person's heart and not what they were wearing or driving? What if you did not automatically dismiss the person who had children? What If you married the geek, lame or quirky person? What if the height or the neighborhood where they lived did not matter?

Let me share four personal relationship stories with you of how decisions in love relationships can affect your entire world.

During my high school and undergraduate school years, my male best friend and I had a purely platonic relationship. I was 15 years old, and he was 17 years old. We attended the same high school, he lived on the same block as the Phillips family and as fate would have it, we attended the same college. We were best friends. We shared similar interests and passions. He was my buddy, and we could talk all night and hang out all day. When he and I met, he was in leadership at his local church. He was incredibly talented and intelligent. He was the first male to take me on a "date". It was at a TGIF restaurant. We drove there in a cab when I was in the 10th grade. My friend loved the theater and Broadway. He purchased my first concert ticket to go with him to see Whitney Houston at Madison Square Garden. He took me to see the Broadway play, 'Dream Girls', starring Jennifer Holliday. We worshiped in the same Christian group in high school and in college. If you saw me, somewhere nearby you saw my friend. We shared laughable moments. I have fond memories of our friendship. We had the best friendship anyone could have between two people of the opposite sex. We were young, but the connection was obvious.

I was taught that you should marry your best friend and that being best friends first makes a successful marriage. At that time, I could see him as a future mate. After some time it seemed he and I were well on our way to a great marriage. Without hesitation, I would have married him if he had asked me, even in college. Nonetheless, there was no proposal. I graduated from college, met, and started dating my first boyfriend post-college. One day my best friend of seven years phoned me to share that he was not attending any one particular church and was exploring a relationship with someone of the same sex. Now, it all made sense to me, the pieces to the puzzle fit and now I knew why he could not commit to a romantic relationship with me and kept me in the "friend zone". My friend said that this was his truth and that it was his path to follow. I could not change who he was or who he was physically attracted to. I treasure our friendship and the memories we shared. We have kept in touch over the years, and he will always have a place in my heart because I truly value those years of our earlier friendship. It was strong, loving, respectful, and adventurous as I transitioned from a teenager to a young lady. My dreaming about "us" back then was real, but my friend was honest enough not to lead me down "that" road to nowhere. However, what if he had not followed his truth?

After I graduated from undergraduate school, my first job was working at a group home where I met my first love. This person and I were co-workers and friends. He was a Christian man, funny, kind, generous, well-liked, educated, ambitious, goal-oriented, family-oriented, and loved sports. He was everything I thought my friend was looking for in a man and I wanted to introduce him to her because I did not believe in dating co-workers. I noticed that he was asking me more times than usual to go out to lunch with him or he would sometimes surprise me and bring lunch to my location. I just thought he was being nice because he was my office buddy. One day I shared with him that I wanted him to meet a friend of mine. That is when he finally told me that he had been trying to get my attention for the last two months because he liked me and wanted us to date. I literally start laughing because here I was trying to play matchmaker with someone who just revealed that he wanted to date me. All the friendly gestures and lunch outings were ploys to get my attention. I even told him that I did not date people that I worked with. That is when he informed me that he had gone to Human Resources to put in his resignation. He would soon no longer be employed here.

He and I dated for approximately a year and a half. During this time, he lavished me with gifts, jewelry, clothes, and entertainment that I had never experienced before. Remember, my biological father was never consistently in my life, so here is a man putting his love in words and actions by providing me with expensive things. I actually still have a pearl necklace that he bought for me one Christmas. He was my buddy with a charismatic personality; he got along with everyone and everyone seemed to like him and enjoy his company. A few times we even discussed a future together. However, I was just enjoying the relationship.

He taught me how to drive a manual transmission, which was the first vehicle that I purchase after I graduated from college. This is a skill I have never lost. One laughable moment that I will never forget during my relationship with him is going to the theater to see the movie, 'I'm Gonna Git You Sucka'! Honestly, I thought the movie theater attendant was going to kick us out. We laughed out loud so hard, tears were running down my face and I was holding my stomach screaming laughing. From teaching me new things to fun outings, we were enjoying each other's company. However, in the midst of this fun-loving relationship I had a dream that I shared with my close friend, Marion. I dreamed that both of our boyfriends left us to marry someone else. We laughed because, at that time, Marion and I knew we were in a promising relationship. I told Marion that, "Time will Tell the Story".

One day, I was visiting him and noticed a card in the distance. He had left the room for a moment. Curious, I walked over to the dresser, picked the card up, and inside the otherwise blank card, someone had written all the words to the late Whitney Houston song, 'Didn't we almost have it All'! When he entered back into the room, I inquired about the person who signed the card. He shared with me that the author of the card was his first love in college. They had a serious relationship and she became pregnant. He was a football player and in a fraternity and she was in a sorority, and could sing. Both were popular on campus. They made the decision to terminate the pregnancy. They both later regretted the decision. There were many emotional repercussions that left them angry, confused, and questioning their love. As a result, they broke up and transferred to other schools. The card was just the tip of the entire story.

After their breakup, both of them pursued other relationships and had not communicated in years. After his "ex" from college ended an engagement with another man, she reached out to him hoping that they could finally bring closure to their breakup and pursue love again. I realized at that moment that I had to make a decision to "fight for love" or let my relationship go. Standing before me was a man whose heart was still with his first love although over the years he had engaged in at least four other relationships before meeting me. The problem was that he was still in love with someone else. I did not want him to have any regrets in his life. What If, he did not have a chance to pursue and rekindle his love with his college sweetheart? What If I fought for our relationship and won but he looked at me one day and regretted that he did not have the opportunity to find out if he still loved his ex from college. What If, I let him go and trusted in the saying that, "If he is meant for you, he will return?" The years had not diminished his thoughts of what if they had both remained at that college and remained in close proximity, maybe it would have brought closure.

What If, I did not want to wait or place my life on hold for him to decide who he wanted to be with? My mind was filled with What Ifs but I had to be true to my heart and character. I broke up with him. I released him to explore a second chance with his college lover. After all, she was the person who would have made him a father six years earlier and apparently was asking herself some What Ifs. He could not believe that just like that, I was giving up our relationship and would not agree to stick around to see if they would make it work. Just six months later, after we moved on, I received a telephone call from him and his fiancé. He wanted to inform me of their engagement and she wanted to thank me for "letting him go" and not attempting to prevent him from pursuing a renewed relationship with her. I gave them my blessings, and to my knowledge, they have been married for almost 29 years, have successful careers, and three daughters. What if I had waited to see what would happen?

By the time I received the above telephone call I had met my "Knight in shining armor". Everyone in my inner circle knows who this man is by name!!! He was a minister at his local church. This man was the epitome of chivalry being alive and well! He came from a two-parent household in which his father modeled before him how a man should treat a woman and provide for his family. He treated me like a queen! My father once told me when I was a little girl that he named me Regina because I was a queen! May-be this guy was my King? He opened the doors, took me by the hand to assist me in the car, and reminded me not to open the car door before he had a chance to come to help me get out. I know that if there were a puddle of water from the rain he would carry me or put his coat down so my feet would not get wet. He would not let me lift a bag or any heavy objects. He actually moved me from one apartment to another and refused to let me carry a plate. He would send flowers to my job for no other occasion but to let me know that he loved me and was thinking about me. He even purchased gifts and flowers for my mother. My friends wanted to know if he had any brothers! He always drove us to our outings, events, and dates even when I wanted to share the responsibilities. He refused to let me spend my money on a date even if I offered to pay or suggested going Dutch. I could only spend my money if something was purchased in advance without his knowledge and/or I was surprising him. He actually gave me a surprise 25th birthday party that he organized with my family and close friends. I know that this man not only spoiled me but loved me and would do anything to please me. He was the perfect gentlemen. I know you are wondering, well what happen to Mr. Right?

Mr. Right, unfortunately, came into my life when I was attending Graduate school. At this time, I had a checklist that included, a man with a college degree. Mr. Right only had one attempted semester of college and was determined not to pursue a degree. He was a hard worker but I did not see him as ambitious enough for me. He was working as a security guard at a bank. I had a salary job and he only made hourly wages. He lived with his parents and I had my own apartment. Maybe I could compromise and make this relationship work. However, the real barrier for me with Mr. Right was that he could not intellectually stimulate me. We were on different levels. He could not engage in day-to-day conversation with me to discuss current events. He struggled to express his thoughts unless we were discussing the Bible or food. He wanted to marry me but at that time, I could not see a future with Mr. Right! His parents were relocating out of New York. He wanted to move with them and asked me to give up Graduate school. My employer was paying for my education and I had no desire to move away from my family and friends. I knew that I would not have been happy so I declined his offer. I noticed that he allowed his parents to influence his decisions and they had a tight rein over his life. At times I felt that he didn't have a "backbone" which frustrated me and I knew eventually that I would not honor him.

After his parents left New York, a month later he also moved to be close to them. I saw him once in 1996 when he came to visit me in Ohio after I had relocated there. He shared with me that his parents would not be happy if they knew he came to see me. He was nervous the entire time. Since that visit, we have not communicated. However, I am still in contact with one of his family members that informed me that he has been married twice, pastored two churches, and has no children of his own. What if I did not have a checklist waiting for one man to fulfill all of my desires? I was young and foolish operating in this world's Kingdom instead of God's Kingdom, doing things his way. Mr. Right was a believer and in hindsight, I must admit that we did have more things in common, plenty of things we agreed on even more than my two previous significant relationships. See, the man of my "dreams" on that checklist had to have a college degree, make more money than me, and be able to engage in conversations with me on every subject. What If I married Mr. Right who made an honest living who told me that if he had to work three jobs to provide and make me happy he would? What If I transferred to a college in a new town to spend my life with a good man who loved me? Could I have become the First Lady? I realized that I ended a relationship with a good man with the influence of others telling me that I would not be happy with a man not on my socioeconomic level or intellectual level. What If they were wrong? What If I understood then that love is more important than money? What If I did not convince myself that he was not good enough for me?

A year after my relationship ended with Mr. Right, I met my children's father. He was tall, dark and handsome! I was physically attracted to him and I knew that from the moment I laid eyes on him at my church while he was singing in the visiting church's choir. He was my sweet temptation and I had a sweet tooth for chocolate! In addition, I thought he was a fulfillment of a prophecy spoken over my life six years earlier. When I was 20 years old a man of God prophesied to me saying that "the Lord showed him that I would get married at age 27". Surely, my children's father was my husband because I met him at age 26 and he wanted to get married two weeks after we met. However, I just wanted to get to know him first on an intimate level and not discuss marriage since we had just met. I wanted to dive into our "Season of Embracing" and take our time developing a steady relationship. I would see if he was the second missing Mr. Right.

It turns out that I did not get married at 27 years old. I delivered our first baby girl and three years later, after a one and a half year break up and a "one night stand", at 30, I conceived again. It was another girl. We were never married. However, we brought two beautiful girls into this world. They are the apple of my eye! My Pride and Joy! The reason my heartbeats! I am blessed to be their mother! No one could have told me that I would have had two children out of wedlock. I was convinced at age 13 when I gave my life to Christ, that I would be a virgin on my wedding night, have this ideal marriage, and plan a family. By the age of twenty-six, I had two opportunities to get married, one was to Mr. Right and the other was to my children's father. In December 1996 I made the choice to end the relationship with their father and not engage in another committed relationship. I chose to raise my children alone. It was important to me as a parent to provide my daughters with a stable home filled with love, peace, protection, guidance, activities, celebrations, discipline, support, and encouragement. My desire was not only to teach and instill morals and values in them but more importantly, to set a godly example for them. I am Thankful that God gave me the strength and grace to raise my daughters and I am extremely Proud of the beautiful ladies that they have become! Unfortunately, just like me, my daughters did not have a consistent relationship with their father. He undoubtedly loved his girls, however; he was incapable of being a part of their daily lives because he refused to address his physical and mental health issues. Sadly, he transitioned from this life in January 2020. Our girls were blessed to have several good men in our "village" to be positive male role models to them.

Solomon wrote a love poem to show the passion of lovers and their feelings about each other which eventually lead to marriage. Solomon shows that when true love radiates between couples, their friends rejoice and are happy for them. I want to challenge you to read 1 Corinthians 13:4 -8 (NIV). Those scriptures give you a true understanding of what Agape love is. After reading them I ask you to substitute the word love for your mate's name. Does it fit the biblical definition of love? For example, the scripture says that "Love is patient and kind. Love is not jealous or boastful or proud or rude. It does not insist on its own way; it is not irritable or resentful, but rejoices in the truth… Love never ends." Can you say that about your mate? Is he or she patient and kind? Is he or she jealous, boastful, or rude? Does he or she insist on having their own way?

Do you ever wonder about your decisions when choosing a mate or dating someone? It has been said that the right person will come into your life if you let the wrong person go. What If you chose the other option? Recently, I watched the 25th Season of the Bachelor Show. It was around the sixth week that a young lady showed up at the location where the show was airing wanting a chance to meet the Bachelor after a mutual friend of this young lady and the Bachelor told her that she would be the perfect mate for the Bachelor. This young lady drove miles to meet the Bachelor, quarantine in a hotel, and then made her unannounced appearance to the Mansion to a Rose Ceremony. Most people thought she was crazy and needless to say, the other women on the show, who had already begun fighting for the love, attention, and time of the Bachelor, were absolutely livid! However, the unexpected guest did not care about the opinion of others, she was not seeking anyone's approval nor did she care that her approach was unorthodox. She just wanted a chance to meet the star of this season's Bachelor and possibly explore a relationship with him. She was making her own decisions regardless of popular opinion.

When the cameras were rolling, she said that she did not want to regret not taking the chance of meeting the Bachelor. What If she could find love and meet her soul mate? The Bachelor greeted her with opened arms but sent her home basically informing her that she came a little too late, timing was not on their side because he had started developing relationships with other women. The young lady drove off knowing she gave it a try and never have to wonder What If? Lucille Ball once said, "I'd rather regret the things I've done than regret the things I haven't done".

It is my hope and prayer that you seek God concerning relationships. I celebrate all who got it right the first time and married the love of their life! You made a decision and it worked out for you. It is my hope that those of you that are in unhealthy, abusive, unfruitful, and unhappy relationships work on them for improvements even if it means seeking counseling and/ or making the decision to leave and explore other possibilities. I pray for all Single people wanting to marry that God grants you the desires of your heart!

In the four relationships that I mentioned in this chapter, I learned powerful lessons. I was young and made choices based upon previous belief systems. I cannot change the past but I will share with you that I do not have a long checklist now. My values and standards have slightly changed as I matured. Understanding God's Word and how His Kingdom operates is life-changing and now I can make better choices concerning a mate. In the words of Dr. Rod Parsley in Columbus, Ohio, "It's better to miss the "Right one" than to end up with the "Wrong one".

Chapter Six

FRIENDSHIPS

I am going to move away from the romance department for this chapter. This is a short and sweet chapter on the topic of friendship. I remember years ago, Oprah Winfrey said that everyone should have a friend like her best friend, Gayle King, in their lives. I wanted to high-five Oprah from my television screen and say, "Yes, Girl I Do!"

Most people have heard of Maslow's hierarchy of needs. "Maslow's hierarchy of needs is an idea in psychology proposed by Abraham Maslow in his 1943 paper 'A Theory of Human Motivation in the Psychological Review. Basically, Maslow's hierarchy of needs is a motivational theory in psychology comprising a five-tier model of human needs, often depicted as hierarchical levels within a pyramid. From the bottom of the hierarchy upwards, the needs are: physiological (food and clothing), safety (job security), love and belonging needs (friendship), esteem, and self-actualization. Needs lower down in the hierarchy must be satisfied before individuals can attend to needs higher up," (Wikipedia).

According to Maslow's theory, the third level of the hierarchy, after physiological and safety needs have been fulfilled, are social needs and involves feelings of love and belongingness. The need for interpersonal relationships includes friendships, intimacy, trust, acceptance, receiving and giving affection and love. In addition, having an affiliation with neighbors, co-workers, social clubs, worship gatherings, a circle of friends or even gang affiliation serves this purpose. Maslow's theory of psychology put simply, says that people need to feel love, connection, and have a sense of belonging.

No one should feel like they live alone on an island. God wants to connect us to the right people on earth to fulfill our needs for love and belonging. Even Jesus was born into a family and later had twelve disciples that helped with his ministry. God created the world and everything else contained within it. After he formed man from the dust of the earth, God said, it was not good for Adam to be alone, so he took a rib from the man and made woman, Eve. She was made after his own kind, a human not another animal, insect, or tree. Adam was created in the image of God. God did not want Adam to feel lonely. Adam did not know he was lonely because, before the fall of man, he had absolutely no knowledge of anything negative. God knew in advance that it was not good for man to be alone so he gave Adam a woman, a helpmate. It was afterwards when Adam and Eve ate the fruit from the forbidden tree that they experienced all human emotions known to us today, including loneliness.

Most adults decide which groups and people of common interest and goals that they will affiliate with. The Bible is a road map to help guide you in choosing the right people in your lives to bless you and for you to be a blessing to. Sometimes I hear young people say that they do not have friends. I then ask them, how have you shown yourself friendly to your peers? Have you offered a proper greeting, a smile, a handshake, introduced yourself, spoke to them first, sat with them during lunchtime to engage in conversation, offer to assist them with a project or homework? We live in a society today that most introductions go like this: "Hey can I DM you", "What's your social media name", "let me put my number in your phone". God's Word says that if you want friends you must be friendly, (Proverbs 18:24).

There are so many scriptures on friendships in the Old and New Testament, but I will only point out a few that helped me make the best decisions. The Word helped me know who to befriend, choose as peers and look to for mentorship in diverse cultures and ethnicities. I have a handful of friends that have been in my life. Many of my friendships have lasted twenty to over forty-plus years. There were a few friendships in my past that did not hold up during the test of time. But God knew that those people were in my life for a reason, a season, and not meant to stay for a lifetime. The Bible holds examples of every kind of friendship.

I share my thoughts with you on this topic because I always saw myself as a friendly person. (Well, I must confess, since it is good for the soul, I was a little bullish in elementary school. I did not have a lot of fistfights but I did my share of teasing others and making a few kids bring me candy to school. Now if you are reading this and you are one who I imitated or scared, please accept my apology. I was a "bae bae" child back in elementary school. However, I put away those childish behaviors in elementary school and was redeemed and set free in middle school). I have gone out of my way to be friendly because I know this to be an excellent asset to have.

I make friends easily with my bubbly and big personality, sense of humor, and being kind-hearted. I really try to show the love of God to people and to see others the way Christ sees them. I have never been a part of a clique or hung out regularly with the same group of people. I tend to get along with others and if it is possible, follow peace, not strife or discord, with all men and women! Others have referred to me as the "life of the party". I just enjoy meeting people, conversing, laughing, and having a good time. I was voted by my senior class in high school, "Most Friendliness, Most Reliable and Most Likely to Succeed". In addition, I was nominated for "Most Popular and Most School Spirit". All thanks to my high school classmates of 1984 for the nominations and votes in the senior superlatives. Honestly, I was not present when the nominations and voting took place at school. As a matter of fact, I was unaware that the votes were happening that day and found out the next day from classmates that I had won in those three categories.

I forgive easily and readily, do not hold on to offenses, or keep a record of wrongdoings. I do not let the sun go down on my wrath and most importantly, I know that my fight is not with the "physical person" but the wrong spirit bothering the person and that I have the authority to rebuke, cast out, and put under my feet that spirit so that change can take place.

I have shared my upbringing with people and some have asked me if I forgave my parents for their wrongdoing and neglect towards me. Of course, I did! I had to forgive them for me, even when my mother denied that events happened and my father did not even ask to be forgiven. It was the love of Christ to forgive and his power that lives inside of me that is greater than any force in the world (I John 4:4). This was the only way I had the ability to forgive any wrongs done to me.

I learned to forgive seventy times seven a day (Matthew 18:21-22) because I need Christ to forgive my sins daily! My first spiritual father in the gospel told me at age 14 that GOD showed him that I do not hold grudges. He was right about that one! How can you say, you love God who you have not seen and hate your brothers and sisters that you do see (I John 4:20)? I came to understand, at an early age, the truth of God's Word not to put confidence in people because they are human and are capable of failing you, disappointing you, and letting you down. Thus, you are not perfect and neither is your family and friends. Now, let us be clear, Jesus requires us to forgive so we can be forgiven. Matthew 6: 14-15 (NLT) says, "If you forgive those who sin against you, your heavenly Father will forgive you. But if you refuse to forgive others, your Father will not forgive your sins." You may not forget how a "friend" hurt you, betrayed you, talked about you behind your back, or attempted to assassinate your character. It is your choice to decide if you want to remain in fellowship with that "frenemy", continues to associate with them, or rebuild the friendship.

Paul and Barnabas, two powerful men in the Bible, who both were involved in great Kingdom work, once had such a disruptive altercation that they had to separate from one another (Acts 15:39). The reality is that not everyone will like you and you will not mesh well with everyone for various reasons and that is alright. Embrace friends who celebrate you, not tolerate you. You do not get to choose your family but you do get to choose your friends, so choose them carefully. The scriptures give us a guideline to help us in finding the right people to befriend. The New Living Translation version of the Bible gives some poignant descriptions of friendships that for me explain somewhat clearer what is meant than earlier translations. Reading episodes in the Bible will enlighten you on ways to make peace with others and how God orchestrates ways for people to meet.

Here are some scriptures from the New Living Translation of the Bible regarding your relationships with others:

• Luke 6: 31 says, "Do to others as you would like them to do to you."

• Colossians 3:12-14 reads, "Since God chose you to be the holy people he loves, you must clothe yourselves with tenderhearted mercy, kindness, humility, gentleness, and patience. 13 Make allowance for each other's faults, and forgive anyone who offends you. Remember, the Lord forgave you, so you must forgive others. 14 Above all, clothe yourselves with love, which binds us all together in perfect harmony."

- Proverbs 18:24 reads, "There are "friends" who destroy each other, but a real friend sticks closer than a brother."

- Proverbs 17:17, "A friend is always loyal, and a brother is born to help in time of need."

- Philippians 2: 3, "Don't be selfish; don't try to impress others. Be humble, thinking of others as better than yourselves."

- Galatians 6:2, "Share each other's burdens, and in this way obey the law of Christ."

- Proverbs 16:28, "A troublemaker plants seeds of strife; gossip separates the best of friends."

- Ecclesiastes 4: 9- 12, "Two people are better off than one, for they can help each other succeed. If one person falls, the other can reach out and help. But someone who falls alone is in real trouble. Likewise, two people lying close together can keep each other warm. But how can one be warm alone? A person standing alone can be attacked and defeated, but two can stand back-to-back and conquer. Three are even better, for a triple-braided cord is not easily broken."

- Proverbs 27:5-6, "An open rebuke is better than hidden love! Wounds from a sincere friend are better than many kisses from an enemy."

- Proverbs 12:26, "The godly give good advice to their friends; the wicked lead them astray."

- Job 16:20-21, "My friends scorn me, but I pour out my tears to God. I need someone to mediate between God and me, as a person mediates between friends."

- Proverbs 27:17, "As iron sharpens iron, so a friend sharpens a friend."

- Proverbs 22: 24-25, "Don't befriend angry people or associate with hot-tempered people, or you will learn to be like them and endanger your soul."

- I Corinthians 15:33, "Don't be fooled by those who say such things, for "bad company corrupts good character."

- Proverbs 13:20, "Walk with the wise and become wise; associate with fools and get in trouble."

- James 4:11, "Don't speak against each other, dear brothers and sisters."

Below is a simple prayer to ask God to bless you with the right friends:

Lord I come before your throne, humbly asking that you place the right people in my life to be my friends; Friends that I can be a blessing to and they can bless me. It is not your will that I am alone. I have a need to be loved and belong. You gave your only begotten Son, Jesus a family, and friends to help complete your Will on Earth. Grant me friends that I can confidant in, share my life with and celebrate special occasions with. Bless me with friends that can help me grow and learn. Encourage me, uplift me, pray for me and support my endeavors. Friends that I can be authentic with and they still love me beyond my faults, Amen!

Choose your friends wisely. If you have a "friend" in your circle who seeks to kill your spirit, plans, and dreams, steal your joy, peace, and happiness and destroy your character and what you are trying to build and develop, then ask yourself is that a person that God portrays as a friend? When you let go of the wrong friends then you make a way for the right ones to come into your path! Unfortunately, most people will experience a "Judas" in their life. Judas comes in disguised as your friend but has other motives and intends to betray you, curse you and cause you pain and sorrow. You may not recognize the "Judas" right away but remain watchful and prayerful. The real person will show up and be exposed in due season for who they really are! Be prepared to release them and let them go! Jesus had to have a disciple betray him to lead him to the cross. The Judas in your life will sell you out for a piece of silver- lust, greed, pride, gossip, envy, and jealousy. The Judas in your life will not get the satisfaction they desire because God will allow you to rise up in their face. He will prepare a table before you in the presence of your enemies! Just remember, in the words of Dr. Maya

Angelou, "When someone shows you who they are, believe them the first time."

There may be a perception issue on your part. You may have to change your views so that you do not limit yourself or your decisions. What If you did not "judge a book by its cover"? What if you got out of your comfort zone and attended events "out of the box" to meet new people in different arenas? What if you did not listen to the opinion or experience of others concerning a person and you got to know them for yourself? What If you apply God's Word when selecting friends?

There are great examples of people in the Bible that had great friendships for you to follow as examples. Abraham and Lot (Genesis 14:14-16) show you the loyalty in a true relationship. Abraham goes above expectations to rescue a friend/relative from captivity. Ruth and Naomi (Ruth 1:16-17) looked out for one another throughout their lives. David and Jonathan (I Samuel 18: 1-3) instantly became friends and made a promise to always look out for each other's best interest. In the story of David and Abiathar (I Samuel 22:22-23) David felt the pain of his friend's loss and vowed to protect him against his enemy. David and Nahash's (ll Samuel 10:2) relationship shows the compassion of a friend when one loses a loved one. David and Ittai (II Samuel 15:19-21) were loyal until the end. David's friendship was unconditional and he did not expect anything in return. Although undiscerning, Job's friends came to comfort him when he had lost everything. When Job faced the greatest adversity in his life, his friends were there to listen. Esther and Mordecai were family. Mordecai raised his cousin and gave her wisdom and instruction to deliver their people. Elijah and Elisha were close friends. Elisha would not let Elijah leave without receiving what he needed from him. The three Hebrew boys went into a fiery furnace together but all came out not burned or smelling like smoke.

You need friends that will go with you to hell and back, be with you through the test, trials, and ups and downs of life. The relationship between Jesus and the siblings, Mary, Martha, and Lazarus was genuine. They could speak candidly and honestly and remain friends. Friends are created more for bad times than they are for the times when you are doing well. You need friends to lift you up and hold you up when you get weary. Aaron and Hur held up Moses' hands when the Israelites were in battle and Moses became weary (Exodus 17:12).

I want to close this chapter with this final scripture, Job 42:10 (NLT), "When Job prayed for his friends, the Lord restored his fortunes. In fact, the Lord gave him twice as much as before!" Always pray for your friends. What you make happen for others in word and deed, God will return to you. Rejoice with your friends when they rejoice and weep with them when they weep. If you want friends, you must show yourself friendly. Be the person that attracts others to your friendly disposition.

The only friend that you can trust, rely and depend on that would not let you down is Jesus. He is a friend that sticks closer than any brother or sister. He is always with you. He does not have a cell phone but you can talk to him anytime. He is always listening and close to your heart. He does not have a social media account but you can count on him. Once you understand the nature and characteristics of Jesus, it will help you be a better friend as you duplicate what you learn from your relationship with Jesus Christ.

Chapter Seven

CAREERS AND CALLINGS

You heard it said before that, "A man's gift makes room for him," (Proverbs 18:16 (NKJV). God created you to be known for your gift that he placed in you. Your gifts and talents are what the world will make room for. Because they are designed by God, your gift will fulfill the plan and purpose for your life. God says to stir up your gifts and talents. It is up to you to cultivate your gifts. Your gift will help you find fulfillment and satisfaction in life. The end of Proverbs 18:16 says, "A man's gift...brings him before great men". The world will pay you for your gift. After you discover what your gift is and develop it, your gift will become a commodity.

God never said that education will make you successful but your gift will! Your gift will make money for you if you do what you were born to do. I believe that having a college degree will give you options in employment but your gift is the key to your success. A person can have a college degree but most likely if they are not in a career that is exercising their gift, they will probably be unhappy, tired, frustrated, angry, stressed, and depressed. God told Joshua to meditate on His Word, do everything according to the law and He would make him prosperous and have good success. (Joshua 1:8). I shared with you earlier that God has a Kingdom, His way of doing things. God gifted you with talents before you were conceived. There is a place for you in this world and someone is waiting for the manifestation of your gift to pay you for it.

There is an array of celebrities and famous people who never went to college but used their gifts to become successful. The following are just the name of a few, Eddie Murphy was born in New York. His father left the family, his brother Charlie and his mother when Eddie was three. His father was killed when he was eight. Shortly thereafter his mother became ill and Eddie and his brother Charlie did a year in foster care. It was here where Eddie honed his comedic skills. He started doing standup as a teenager, causing him to almost not graduate high school. His mother made him go to summer school. Eddie went on to do the club circuit until he landed a spot on the sketch comedy television show Saturday Night Live. The rest is history (WWW.Biography.com). Ryan Gosling came from a working family in Canada where he was raised in the Church of Jesus Christ of the Latter-Day Saints. At a young age, he landed a spot on a Disney show. That lasted for two years. That was just the beginning of his acting career. He starred in many other shows and movies, even one starring alongside Denzel Washington (WWW>Biography.com). Lastly, I want to mention Whoopi Goldberg. She did drop out of high school, but before that, she saw a black actress with a role on Star Trek. She became enamored with Star Trek when she realized that African Americans could have parts other than maids.

Her name looms large in entertainment as her gift for comedy gave her a great start even without the benefit of a degree. As you see, some celebrities not only ever attended college, but some never finished high school.

Becoming wealthy is not based on your pedigree. As you can see from the previous paragraph, some people obtain wealth by honing their gifts and talents. I will take liberties to just insert some biblical truths. God did choose, call and make a covenant with several of His servants in the Bible to be or become wealthy. In addition, some people are simply born into wealth. In the Old Testament, Abraham, Isaac, Jacob, and Job were extremely rich, just like Solomon, Joseph, Ruth, and the Queen of Sheba. The following are people in the New Testament that were wealthy believers who gave generously to those in need. From the scriptures indicated by their names you can read about their lives: Joseph called Barnabas (Acts 4: 36-37), Dorcas (Acts 9:36), Cornelius (Acts 10:1) Sergius Paulus (Acts 13:6-12), Jason (Acts 17:5-9), Aquila and Priscilla (Acts 18:2-3), Mnason of Cyprus (Acts 21:6) and Philemon (Philemon 1).

God has given you gifts and talents to prosper you. Deuteronomy 8:18 reminds us that, "God gives us the power to get wealth, that He may establish His covenant." In addition, God can give you one idea to change your life forever. Ultimately, you have to discover and develop your gifts to bring you success. Chose a career where your gifts will flourish and bring you success. You will find it very rewarding when you are using your natural abilities in a field that makes you happy, fulfilled and financially prosperous.

I have seen and heard about people who are working in jobs where they are not the right fit. Believers have to know their gifts and talents and where they fit even in the body of Christ which is the church. Scripture tells you that everyone cannot be the head in the body of Christ. Some people are the fingers or the toes. There is no part of the body of Christ more important than the other. Each part has its function in the body and if everyone finds their place, it will all operate properly. If one part of the body is dismembered then the body cannot function properly. We need you, as a member in the body of Christ, to know your part, where you fit and operate so we can all be fitly joined together and have a strong church. I believe that this also applies in the secular arena. If everyone discovers their gifts and talents and operates in their purpose, can you imagine what kind of world we would have?

There are people who are working in the health profession that don't care for all people. Their gift is really in the technology field. There are people not happy with their jobs because they are not exercising their gifts and talents in the right field. There are preachers and pastors who do not love the people of God as they should in the pews but like the applause of the crowd, title, or financial gain from them; they should be driving trucks or doing something else. Just think of all the careers and positions that we have in the world and then imagine everyone working in careers according to their gifts and staying in their "lane". Everything would work together and we would be a strong progressive nation. America would be in better shape because everyone would have a moral aptitude for serving others. People would have a better attitude toward each other. Everyone would be resting comfortably in what God called and equipped them to do.

I want to encourage you not to miss opportunities to grow, develop and pursue your gifts. The world not only needs your gifts and talents but they will make room for you. Do not be like the man who hid his one gift/talent in the ground (Matthew 25:18). What if you would have chosen the career of your passion? What if you had applied for the position to expand your career? What if the world is still waiting for your gift to be displayed? What if you are the next inventor of something great? What if you got over your fears and stirred up the gifts that are in you to fulfill your purpose? It is never too late to go back to school to obtain your education. If your gift is in a field that education can advance you to pursue your passions, why not? What If you obtained your college degree?

I am doing well now, but it has not always been that way. I was retained in the 7th grade after missing numerous days of school from September to March of my first year in middle school. Neither parent was actively involved in my education. My father never attended any of my Parent-Teacher conferences and my mother only attended two during my enrollment in elementary school. My parents never checked my homework or even asked me about my school day. I recall my father occasionally asking to see my Report Card if it was available at the times he would visit with us. In hindsight, I believe my mother viewed school as a safe place for me to attend while she worked during the day. I literally lived across the street from the middle school and when I attended it was always late. I would gather up the "cut class" notifications in the mailbox and trash them before my mother arrived home from work. She never asked me about school so the message was that she wasn't interested in my education. From 1978-1979 I was also addicted to the television soap opera General Hospital. General Hospital was a popular show when I was in seventh grade. Luke, Laura, and Scotty's drama was my main focus and a reason to rush home after the last class to get a snack and get comfortable to watch my show from 3 – 4 pm.

When I accepted Christ into my life on March 11, 1979, he made all the difference in every area of my life. He gave me a new disposition and outlook on life. I desired to be a "Light" in the world. I was a leader amongst my peers in all the wrong things before being born again. I remember trying my first cigarette at age 11, wanting desperately to make the "ring smoke" design when I exhaled because after watching others do it I thought it was so cool. I could not learn how to make the cigarette circles or learn to inhale so I gave that up quickly. I had my first puff of marijuana at age 12 and a few times after that, but that experience didn't last long either because I did not have money to buy it. I used it with my friends who received it from a supplier in my "hood". After "using" everything seemed funny and then we would have the munchies. I would play pranks on neighbors by ordering food to their homes and watching their reaction when the delivery person showed up at their door. My friends and I would go to nearby apartment buildings and ring on doorbells and run. My brother and I would have a stream of traffic of friends going in and out of our apartment on the weekends. We would do whatever we wanted to because we had no boundaries, no rules, and no parental supervision.

My father wasn't present and my mother worked hard all week and lived her "Best Life" on the weekends. We maybe saw my mother twice between Friday night and Saturday morning. She came home in enough time to shower and change her clothes again, then back out she went. She always made sure that we had a key to get back into the apartment and she kept food in the house for us to eat. My father never verbally corrected me for any wrongdoing that he became aware of nor did he ever lay hands on me for discipline. That's probably why I never had a physically abusive relationship because my mentality with men was; my father never hit me, and baby you won't either.

In my upbringing, I only received two whippings and they were both from my mother. If she was upset about something, she would yell and her screams went in one ear and out the other. Trust me, I knew as a child that I deserved consequences for my actions. Even when the neighbors, my "Village" or the staff at the elementary school reported negative behaviors to my mom she would listen then makeup excuses for my actions and never implemented any consequences. So I learned at an early age that I could do and say anything I wanted to and get away with it because my parents did not enforce any consequences. I had to learn the importance of respecting, obeying and submitting to those that had rule over me.

I recall going to Friendly's Ice Cream store in the neighborhood and plotting with my friends to steal the tips off the table. One of them would distract the workers by asking questions, while the rest of us stole the tips off the table, and then we would walk back up to the cash register and order ice cream. My parents were not involved in my life so when the wrong behavior was brought to their attention they did not hold me accountable. They had no clue of the peer pressures that I had experienced or succumbed to at an early age. They never talked to me about relationships, puberty, personal hygiene and grooming, boys, sex, friendships, the importance of education, death, drugs, alcohol, coping skills, and all the topics that parents should have with their children. I did some things in my childhood that I regret because my parents didn't teach me right from wrong.

Some of my right or wrong decisions were made because the voice of my conscience was alive. For example, I can recall going into a store to buy a pair of jeans. Yes, my parents would give me money, and I had the liberty to shop in New York by myself. I rode public transportation there and back. I was about ten or eleven years old. I grabbed a pair of jeans and went into the fitting room to try them on. There was a pair of gold earrings on the floor and something told me to steal them, but I heard another voice saying for me not to take them. I was in that fitting room for about twenty minutes thinking of all the pros and cons if I took the earrings and got away with stealing them or if I got caught stealing. I decided to leave the earrings on the floor. My parents never told me that it was "wrong" to steal or take things that did not belong to me. They did not instill any values or morals in me. What they modeled was work ethics and staying true to you.

Accepting Christ in my life and walking in newness of life was exciting to me. I wanted to change my life and learn new ways of doing things. As you can see, at an early age I was heading down a road of destruction before Christ saved me from myself. What If Yeshua had not saved me when he did? I literally at the time had friends that told me that I was too young for salvation; I needed to have fun and a good time before becoming "a holy roller"! Unfortunately, some of those same friends, dropped out of school, landed in detention centers, became teen parents, and struggled with substance abuse. All I can say about their journey and the choices some of them made is, "There I go, but by the Grace of God!"

I started attending school on a regular basis and turning in my assignments on time. However, it was too late to redeem myself because I had missed too many days of school. Therefore, I was retained and had to repeat 7th grade. After graduating from middle school and entering high school in my freshmen year, I developed a plan with my Guidance Counselor to earn all the necessary credits to graduate in three years with my original class of 1984 as if I had not to be retained in 7th grade. I was motivated to do whatever it took to graduate in three years.

After we completed my schedule, to my amazement, my Caucasian counselor looked at me and expressed her concerns and disbelief that I could follow through with the plan. She suggested that after high school I attend a business or trade school like my older sister Michele did. At that moment, I realized that I had more to prove. It wasn't just about me accomplishing my goals but letting this lady know that she stereotyped the wrong black girl. Her doubtfulness and remarks put a "fire" in my feet and I was more determined to prove her wrong and settle her disbeliefs. Needless to say, it was this Guidance Counselor that had to deliver me the news that not only had I completed all my high school credits in three years and was now eligible to graduate, but I had received community awards. There was not only a special seat for me to sit in at the Senior Award Ceremony but I had been accepted to Hofstra University on a full scholarship!!!!

I was attending a church where the Pastor, Bishop Ronald H. Carter, and his wife, Dr. Phyllis Carter were the Overseers. They valued education and encouraged young people to obtain a higher level of education. My Pastor had the "Ronald H. Carter" fund where he would proudly give a dollar to all the kids who made honor roll each quarter. That still makes me laugh. I now had a support system at church where and I was surrounded by leaders who valued education and taught us that a "Mind is a terrible thing to waste"! There were young people at church who were scholars, gifted and talented. I was affiliated with church members and a Pastor who taught the Word of God from Philippians 4:13 that say, "I Can Do All Things through Christ that strengthens me." At Refuge Church we had members who were both blue- and white-collar workers. I realized that not all blacks lived in the projects and did not have to be products of their environment. You have a choice to pursue a better life for yourself if you were willing to take action and attain happiness.

Recently, I was reminded that in 7th grade, after I gave my life to Christ that I would witness the Gospel in music class. I would share the Good News with anyone who wanted to listen. It was out of that experience that my peers would come to me for support and prayer. I enjoyed listening and helping to solve problems. I wanted to know where and how others can receive assistance in the time of need. It was fulfilling for me to help others. I began to believe that human behavior can change if the person is willing and had the tools they needed. I knew that I wanted a career in the help profession. I may not be able to build a bridge, but I can help build character and help you cross over one! I know God to be a problem solver. There is not one problem that you encounter that does not have a solution. I decided to choose a career that helped others achieve their goals.

Being a part of the process of helping others is rewarding, gratifying, and fulfilling. I am known as the "Resource Queen" among family, friends, and co-workers.

I have two more career goals that I hope to achieve in the near future. What If, I didn't have a positive support system that instilled the value of education? What if I wasn't exposed to a different environment of positive influencers and leaders? What If I did not discover and develop my gifts?

Surround yourself with people of a like-mind. Talk to others in the career you want to pursue? Be realistic with your career goals and be willing to work to achieve them. Remember, your gift will make room for you and somebody is willing to pay you for it!

Chapter Eight

SEASONS DO CHANGE

King Solomon in the Bible wrote about times and seasons in Chapter 3 of Ecclesiastes. As long as you are alive and walking on this earth you will experience many changes in your life. It may be easy to comprehend when speaking about an infant to adulthood. Their changes are quite obvious. The average infant at birth is 21-1/2 inches long and the average for men and women in the United States is 5'9" and 5'4" respectively. That means that you can see their physical changes as it happens. The difference between these physical changes and the changes and seasons mentioned by King Solomon is not obvious. Whether you can visualize them or not, they still take place.

Everything under the heavens has a time and a season. Nothing takes place as a big bang. In the first eight verses of Ecclesiastes 3, King Solomon has a litany of information on the things that change in everyone's lifetime. He wrote this well over thousands of years ago, yet every tidbit of the list is still true today. There is definitely a time to be " 2a time to be born and a time to die, a time to plant and a time to uproot, 3a time to kill and a time to heal, a time to tear down and a time to build, 4a time to weep and a time to laugh, a time to mourn and a time to dance, 5a time to scatter stones and a time to gather them, a time to embrace and a time to refrain from embracing, 6a time to search and a time to give up, a time to keep and a time to throw away, 7a time to tear and a time to mend, a time to be silent and a time to speak, 8a time to love and a time to hate, a time for war and a time for peace (Ecclesiastes 3:2-8 AMP)." This is easy to read and even easier to understand. As long as the earth is part of God's creation, each of these transformations will continue to have their cycles in the life of every human here now and to come later.

It is appointed for every human being to be born and then at a given time to die. For those who are believers in Christ, this is not a negative thought and we have hope beyond the grave, heaven our eternal home. Knowing this must give you a reason to fulfill your purpose on earth during the period called your life on earth. You have a birthdate and then a dash that means much before that end date when you stop breathing. That dash, although not always given much attention, represents years full of transitions, transformations, and on occasion a gigantic metamorphosis. Pay attention to this paragraph because it will make you consider how you spend each day.

You may be one who will do something that you have not seen done before. Never be afraid of being an innovator. In the Bible, it is said that if you practice being wise you will find the knowledge of witty inventions (Proverbs 8:12). At that time there will be opportunities to start something new. By the same token, there will be a time to develop what you already have. Everything has its place in time and it would be wise to tune into what season you are in. Somebody has to be the one to begin something; why not you?

The next phrase in the passage in Ecclesiastes says that there is also a time to kill. You and I both know that this cannot be literal for all generations or territories. You cannot just go out and murder, but you can kill some influences and ways of doing things. There may be people in your life whose advice you no longer benefit from. Kill it and be open for another direction. After the change in perspective, there will be a time to heal. "Many are the afflictions of the righteous: but the Lord delivereth him out of them all (Psalms 34:19 KJV). It can be painful to kill something in your life that you have become accustomed to. But another chapter and verse in psalms lend more support to being afflicted: "It was good for me to be afflicted so that I might learn your decrees (Psalms 119:71 NIV). Go ahead and kill what you need to so that healing can begin.

Added to all of this doing and undoing is also crying and laughing. Throughout life, you will have a time when you are sad and even mourn losses. But, as the old saying goes, "Trouble don't last always!" Keep living and you will walk into the next season. Sadness and crying have their place the same as joy, laughter, and celebration.

Even with all these changes throughout life you still must learn how to be a good steward. What does that mean? When you are living in a prosperous place during joyous times do not be like the prodigal son in the Bible (Luke 15:11-32) and spend up all of your assets without restraints. There will be a time when you will lose and you must prepare for that. If you can have half the wisdom that Joseph had while residing in his season of loss (Genesis 37-50), you will make it through to another season of gaining.

You do not know how good God is until you have experienced the opposite of good. Think about it this way, how do you know what love is without the presence of hate? There are things that you must hate in order to embrace the love of God. If I did not hate that the counselor told me I needed to go to trade school I would never have gone on to graduate and then post-graduate school. Those times of living on the wild side may have been fun at the time, but they definitely were not good. Because of that season, I learned to go after the getting. Yes, it was hard work, but it was worth every minute. I give God all the glory for all the good that he allowed to overtake the bad in my life. Yes, God is really good.

There will always be wars in this life; not only just the catastrophic ones of the country against the country. The wars in your life will come when you want to hold onto something that is no longer right for you. That war will be with you. Your higher self that is tuned in with God will tell your natural self to change. Change is not always easy. You do not want to look back and wonder "What if" I would have changed. How would my life be different? Better to fight the war at the right time than to start a battle out of season.

It would not be fair to discuss war without bringing peace into the conversation. What would your life be like if there was only war? That is why Ecclesiastes 3:8 says that there is a time for war and a time for peace. War would not make sense without peace. When the war for change arises in your life the question you should always ask yourself is, "Why am I fighting?" The answer should always be that you are fighting for peace.

As Christians, you must first understand that God has the power to change your season in due time. Due time is when God says so. No matter where you find yourself in life always remember that God is still in control. Go back a few paragraphs and recall when David wrote in Psalms that it was good that he was afflicted because it was then that he learned God's ways. When you have learned what God is teaching your season will change.

Nothing is permanent except God and his promises. When you look at the life of Joseph in Genesis 37-50 you will find many times of hurt and pain, rejection and loneliness. All of these afflictions worked together for Joseph's greater good. When Joseph was first made aware that he was a dreamer and his faith revealed to him that his dreams would come true, he was a seventeen-year-old immature young man. He bragged about the promotion that God had in store for him. He had no idea what this would take him to. Romans 8:28 says that everything is working together for the good of them that love the Lord and are called for his purpose. Joseph had no clue of what he would have to endure before leading his family to safety. As a matter of fact, all he was told was that he would rise up to be over his family. How or why this would happen was not mentioned. It was for him, his family, and the rest of the world. If it was not for his gift given to him by God, the whole world would have been in trouble. Stuck at the bottom of a pit, slavery and prison time could not stop God's plan. None of them was permanent, but God's promise stood the test of time.

It does not matter what you are going through, no season is permanent and everyone has an expiration date. That is why it is best to trust God and not your own understanding. What you think you know can lead you down a dead-end road. Only your experiences while trusting God can stand the test of time. Even circumstances that seem similar to something can have a different outcome. To put it simply: think about winter in your part of the world. It is never identical to the previous one. The snow days are never the same neither are the days when it is freezing. The only things guaranteed are, God's word and that he is in control of the length of seasons.

Do not get attached even to the good. As good as it may seem, there is another place in God that he will take you. You cannot get there without this season-ending. It is best to embrace the change because only he can get you through everything. Without God, you can do nothing (John 15:5). The only reason why anyone would try to hold onto anything is to prove how great they are, Live in gratefulness and that will take away any sense of independent accomplishment. Good can only get better with God.

As mentioned before, even winter is not the same every year. Maybe you are in a severe winter season. Do not despair. Remember that your season will change. You must endure like a good soldier. Hold on to your freedom in God. God can comfort you no matter where you are in life. Even downtimes can be a time of refreshing because they make room for the next season. Do not anticipate that although your winter will come again, that it will be as bad as the last one.

You can go through a season of unemployment to gainfully employ the next. Maybe you had a family crisis and are behind in your rent or mortgage. That will not always be the case. You could end up in a better apartment or a new home. As long as you continue to move forward your change will come. Transitions are actually waiting on you. God goes behind the scenes and prepares your seasons. You just have to walk into them. Nothing will ever remain stagnant.

You should never make permanent decisions based on temporary situations. This can be tricky because as much as people love stability, things do change. The biggest mistake you can make is to base a decision on how you are feeling. Not only is God changing seasons, but your emotions are also changing. Unfortunately, sometimes your emotions do not coincide with what God is doing. You may get weary before your transition comes. Just boost up your faith and hold on. Your change will come and the temporary flare of emotions will dissipate.

Seasons are changing, but you will still be here. Just like when Moses led the children of Israel out of Egyptian slavery, God killed the entire firstborn to coerce Pharaoh to let the Hebrews leave. God instructed Moses to tell the Israelites to put blood over their doorpost so that the death angel would pass over their dwelling (Exodus 12). No firstborn of the Israelites died that night. This is where the name Passover comes from. This was the first Passover. The death angel passed over them. You will outlast your season if you remain hopeful. Stay prayerful and full of faith. Some children do not see their way out of being bullied. Not even bullying lasts forever. Teach children to speak up. Even you in dire times cannot see your way out. Get some reinforcement. Ask for prayer, see a counsellor, and talk to your pastor or a wise friend. The season will change and you will be there at the end.

God gave specific instructions to Moses on how the children of Israel will make their exodus from Egyptian slavery. You too have to create your strategy. See yourself on the other side of your circumstance. With God, you are stronger than the storm, test, and trials. See yourself living with joy and laughter far away from the mourning and sadness. "Weeping may endure for a night but joy cometh in the morning" (Psalms 30:5). Seasons give us hope that there will be a change.

The negative times are a test of your faith. "If you falter in a time of trouble, how small is your strength (Proverbs 24:10)! "God's strength is made perfect in weakness (2 Corinthians 12:9)." You will make it out of any season because that is God's plan. Expand your faith by looking towards the author and finisher of your faith, God.

Materialist things, friends, and ways of thinking all have an ending. On occasion, you will know that some things and friends must go. Do not even try to hold on to a way of thinking when it is no longer working for you. Cars, houses, clothes, and any other material thing are made in bulk every day. Some friends are here to stay and some were here for a season. Just like Dr. Maya Angelou said, "When you know better you do better." Put an end to the things that can keep you from entering your next season.

Seasons make up a period of time. God created time, but he does not live in it. Time is an interruption in eternity.

God is the only one who can see the end from the beginning. Everything is made beautiful in his time (Ecclesiastes 3:11). Time, like grace, was created for a purpose. You were born to do something with the time that God has given you!

When you understand time and seasons, you won't waste your time on the wrong people, doing the wrong things. It is very easy not to make changes. You can keep doing what you are doing and stay around the same people. You must regularly give yourself a checkup to see if you are where you are supposed to be. As a human, it is normal to be a creature of habit. Sometimes that is the reason why some tests are repeated over and over, you are still taking them the same way. Often passing the test only involves getting away from your current surroundings,

One day in undergraduate school, I was walking around the campus and spotted this shiny gold-plated object on the ground. I picked it up and it was a key chain that read, "I Want it All". That statement rang out loud and clear. I had been thinking about my future after college, whether I was going to return back home to the Phillips family. They had been blessed to move out of the projects in New York and purchase their first house in New Jersey. I needed to decide whether I was going to get my own apartment in New York, what job was I going to pursue, or was going to continue on to get my masters. There were a lot of questions racing in my mind and decisions that I had to make concerning my future. I knew my season was going to eventually change after college, and that reality was creeping up on me. That small chain on the ground was a real message of the status of my thoughts.

I had high hopes and expectations of obtaining a good job with benefits, nice housing, transportation, as well as traveling and enrolling in graduate school. I believed I needed all these things in order to live a productive and self-sufficient life. Yes, I wanted it all and the sky was the limit, but I knew that I had to come up with a plan to move forward. I began to feel a little anxious about my future. I had developed a great work ethic. At age 13, I had my first summer job and worked every summer until graduating from high school. I even worked part-time while attending college. These new thoughts were just a continuation of how I believed after seventh grade and my awakening.

Shortly after finding the key chain and focusing on the present and not the future, I was sitting in my college dormitory room watching the Oprah Winfrey Show when she said something that was an "Aha moment" for me. Oprah had a guest on the show, after the message that was being delivered, she said to the audience, "I get it now, you can have it all but not all at the same time!" That changed my life forever. I began to understand that there are a time and season for everything under the heavens.

You can have what you desire but maybe not all at the same time. You have to pace yourselves, get organized and plan for the next phase of your life. Time was created for a purpose to be fulfilled. The fact that you are still breathing consider what purpose are you fulfilling with your time? What if you didn't make permanent decisions during temporary seasons in your life? There is a time for each thing, and everything has its time. I still have that now rusted and worn key chain.

Chapter Nine

LIFE IS A TRIP – THE CONCLUSION OF THE WHOLE MATTER!

In the New International Version of the Bible Job 14: 1 and 5, reads, "Mortals, born of woman, are of few days and full of trouble. A person's days are determined; you have decreed the number of his months and have set limits he cannot exceed." There is nothing new under the sun. What these words meant thousands of years ago still retain their impact in the 21st Century. Everyone on earth was born by way of a woman. That means you, just like everyone else are here but a few days, and those days are full of trouble. God has determined how long you will be here and you will not be here one year, month, or a day longer.

Although you are here for a short time, it is up to you to make the best of your days. God has given you the authority to choose wisely. Joshua made it clear in Joshua 24:15 that he has chosen for him and his family to serve the Lord. He expressed to those listening that they could go in whatever direction they wanted, but he was making the right choice for him and his family. What sense does it make to use your time pursuing things that will give you temporary pleasure and long-lasting pain? Your time here on earth can be filled with the peace that God sent Jesus on this earth to return to the man.

You must understand that Job lived in a time way before Jesus' physical appearance on the earth. John 10:10 says that Jesus came to give you a full life. The overflowing life was taken from a man in the Garden of Eden after the fall from grace. Not even King Solomon had the ability to have all his time on earth secured by the love God sent on earth through his son Jesus. No, this sinful world cannot give you complete joy. That will not happen until eternity, but you definitely have a better life since Jesus took your sins to the cross. King Solomon found himself believing that all in life was vain (Ecclesiastes 2:1). He was full of wealth and had many women. Near the end of his life he found himself despondent because he found that material possessions could not satisfy; neither could hundreds of wives and concubines. Make the Best of the Time you have on Earth. Everyone has a Sunrise and Sunset date. The journey that you choose is up to you. You have the opportunity than either Job or King Solomon because Jesus can be alive and well in your heart.

Just like Joshua you can make the choice to serve God. With God at the center of your life choosing clothes, spouse, career, and family is an added bonus on earth and afterwards life with God in eternity. The disciples found out about this bonus in Mark 10 after the encounter between the rich young ruler and Jesus. The rich young ruler wanted to gain eternal life so he asked Jesus how he could do that. When Jesus asked him several questions about his life thus far and he answered them affirmatively, Jesus then told him that he lacked one thing. He had too much stuff. This is where some people stop reading. "So now I have to be broke, busted, and disgusted to follow Jesus?" You have to keep reading. The rich young ruler lost out because he was afraid to trust Jesus. He knew enough to come to Jesus to inquire, but he did not like the answer. The disciples then wondered who could be saved. After Jesus explained that all things were possible with God, a light came on in the disciples' heads. They realized that they had left all to follow Jesus. It was at this time that Jesus said the following words, "Truly I tell you," Jesus replied, "no one who has left home or brothers or sisters or mother or father or children or fields for me and the gospel 30 will fail to receive a hundred times as much in this present age: homes, brothers, sisters, mothers, children, and fields—along with persecutions—and in the age to come eternal life (Mark 10:28-29 NIV). You can choose just like Joshua did in the Old Testament and receive the blessings as the disciples did in the New Testament.

You may not be asked to leave your family, but you may have to separate emotionally from some people who are close to you. Anything that is a hindrance in your life should be cut off. Not only can you choose a better life here, but God is also right now preparing even more for your life in eternity.

God has chosen a path just for you. As long as you stick with him he will keep you straight. The road map you choose is simply to follow God. Yes, he is a spirit, but he has a way of speaking to your heart and directing your life. Those that are in a relationship with God will know his voice. When life seems unfair, be sure to check in with God. Not only will he comfort you since he promised never to leave you, but he will take you to the place where it will all balance out. Everyone's path is different, although all believers will end up in the prepared place. Their road there is made to fulfill their destiny. Although it seems unfair, it is fair for their particular calling. Never get caught up in comparison, because it can many times lead to grief. Your house is not as big, you don't make as much money as so and so or your neighbor seems to have it much easier than you. You have no idea of other's full journey. Your path is your path.

Sometimes people make the wrong choice because of insecurities, fears, lack of information, wrong motives, or seeking approval from others. Even these things did not escape God's knowledge. They can turn into lessons or tests. No one lives unto themselves. The main purpose for each life is a relationship with God and the next best one, a relationship with others. How you manage your life is totally up to you. God does not force himself on anyone. Some choices have serious consequences, while others are falling down and get up ones. Remember the words in the passage in Mark 10 that blessing will come, but so will persecutions. Live the best life you can, love God, and give yourself space for mistakes. No one is perfect not even you.

The joy of the Lord is what gives you the strength to continue. Every day is a present and a day that the Lord has made for you to rejoice and be glad. As the late Dr. Martin Luther King, Jr. said, "Longevity has its purpose." He knew. Look at all he accomplished in 39 years on this earth. His life was filled with service to others. He had to know the joy of the Lord.

Unlike Dr. King, when it was time for Hezekiah in the Bible to die, he wasn't ready to leave. He asked for more time (2 Kings 20) and was granted fifteen more years. You can have it either way. But, since you do not know your numbers, it's best to live your best life every day. You do not have to perseverate about what is God's will for your life. You woke up this morning and have twenty-four hours to accomplish something, just like everyone else who is alive and well.

God gave believers another chance through Jesus Christ. Your life should be different than those who live in darkness. Unlike them, you can live in the new life with Christ stands between us and God reconciling what was lost in the Garden. God does not respond to pity parties, only faith. You will constantly miss the mark if you belabor what you do not have and refuse to develop what you have. Don't waste this time and the chance you have been given by Jesus Christ.

Learn to trust the process. Life has its challenges; learn to enjoy the trip. You can do this and God has empowered you to win. The Serenity Prayer has blessed many over the years; its author remains unknown. Serenity involves the qualities of tranquility, peacefulness, calmness, quietness, and stillness to name a few. The Serenity Prayer reads:

God grant me the serenity to accept the things I cannot change, courage to change the things I can, and wisdom to know the difference.

The whole conclusion of man, according to Ecclesiastes 12:13 (KJV) says, "Let us hear the conclusion of the whole matter: Fear God, and keep his commandments: for this is the whole duty of man." Keep life simple, live in the present and forget about the past, embrace the future and anticipate an excellent end!

Forget about what you cannot change. Stop living in the past with all its regrets, shame, mistakes, and What Ifs. You have been set free by the Son of God. God has promised to help you to overcome the sins of your past and leave you with no shame from your younger days. God sent his Son to redeem the world from sin. Everyone that believes in the Son, Jesus Christ, will not go down but have eternal life. Not only should you forget your past, but God has also already put it in a sea that is forgotten. He will not remind you about your past neither will he remember again. (Philippians 3:13 "Brethren, I count not myself to have apprehended: but this one thing I do, forgetting those things which are behind, and reaching forth unto those things which are before...."

God does heal the brokenhearted. Although He is not bringing your sins to your memory, he is very interested in the consequences of your choices. He is in the business of making all things new. The term "God of a second chance" is a misnomer because God gives innumerable chances. You may hear about righteous people falling seven times and then getting up (Proverbs 24:16); seven hear represents God's number of perfection not really just seven. God will heal your heart from every pain you have ever suffered.

Do not go into the future with regrets about, "What ifs "; "should of, could of and would of". You have the opportunity to do it now. Start making better choices today. What if's come when you may have been afraid to act in the past. Change that now. They will taunt you and leave you with regrets causing you to be depressed. You must cast down every vain imagination that torments your mind. These thoughts are against what God said and they attempt to overtake the knowledge of Christ (2 Corinthians 10:5). The bottom line is these thoughts are self-vindicating, half-truths, or lies and are attempts to distract you from the life God has chosen for you to live. Vain imaginations will cause you to engage in fantasy, painful, irrational conversations in your head that is a popular mental sin. These things you have imagined will never happen. Rehearse your new life and do not repeat the vainly imagined one that leaves you busted and disgusted. Do away with the "What ifs".

Practice what it says in Philippians 4:8 (NIV), "Finally, brothers and sisters, whatever is true, whatever is noble, whatever is right, whatever is pure, whatever is lovely, whatever is admirable—if anything is excellent or praiseworthy—think about such things." You only have

113

one life to live and do not have time to be wasted on frivolous thinking or actions that do not bring you peace. Stop imaging other choices and options of all the What if's of the past. You will never know, and those vain imaginations will rob you of your time from embracing the present and stealing your joy. You cannot change the past but accept the life and time you have now to make better choices.

Do everything for God's glory and not man's because in the end it will be God that will ask you to give an account of what you did with your life. It will bring God great joy to say that you have handled your life well and have been the servant he always knew that you could be. Regretful "What ifs" have no place in a life well lived for God.

Closing Prayer

Father, I pray that you bless every man, woman, boy or girl that has read this book. If they are living with regrets, free them from the torment of every unanswered and unknown "why" and "what if " in their mind according to Philippians 4:7 (NIV), "And the peace of God, which transcends all understanding, will guard you hearts and your minds in Christ Jesus". Give them that peace that surpasses all of their understanding. Let them do away with every vain imagination and everything that attempts to elevate itself against the knowledge of God. Bring all negative thoughts to the obedience of Christ and be transformed by the renewing of their mind. Give them the mind of Christ to think on things that are lovely, just, and true and of a good report. Let them receive the victory over the battle in their mind through Christ Jesus our Lord!

Allow decisions that were made by others not to influence the way the reader responds to negative circumstances in their life. Help them not to live with the regrets of "What ifs" because the negative decisions made outside of their control hindered their progress. Lord have mercy on them because of the consequences caused by personal decisions made in error. Let them know that whatever choices that were made, you are in control and it will work out for their good according to your plan and purpose for their lives.

Holy Spirit have control of their life and bless this reader with good friends, and meaningful relationships. Help them to develop their gifts and talents that will bring them success.

Now, may the peace of God be your guide and rest upon you in all your decision-making from now until forevermore!

NOTES

Made in the USA
Monee, IL
10 May 2021